HIGHER POWER HAS A NAME

HIGHER POWER HAS A NAME

BY

CAVANAUGH JAMES

A MILLENNIAL

Inprov, Ltd.
2150 E. Continental Boulevard
Southlake, TX 76092

www.inprov.biz

Distributed by Thomas Nelson

Printed in the United States of America

Edited by Leigh Hickman with additional editing by Leigh Eichhorst

ISBN-13: 978-1-7327904-0-7

DEDICATION

To the ones who have ever felt unseen,
uncared for, or unknown . . .

To the ones who have ever felt too dirty
for grace, too irredeemable for redemption,
and too far away to ever come back home . . .
these pages are for you.

I pray that they would help heal
and suture your heart as only
genuine love can.

FIRST: HONESTY

13

THE HARD CHAPTER

25

THE STRENGTH OF SURRENDER

83

GRACE RECEIVED = GRACE TO GIVE

97

RELATIONSHIPS AND OTHER IDOLS

59

UNMASKING THE LIE OF YESTERDAY
127

LIFE, LIBERTY, AND THE PURSUIT OF PURPOSE
187

RE-SEEING HOW YOU SEE
147

THE ASK
205

TO KNOW AND BE KNOWN
171

Hey there friend!

Before we go any further, there's a tool I want to give you that will help you enjoy this book to its fullest.

Throughout the book, you will find QR codes placed within each chapter. A QR code looks like this:

Your smart phone camera may have a built-in reader to scan this code but if not, no worries ... simply head to the app store on your phone and download a QR reader for free. (If you search for "QR Reader" in the app store, a number of options should come up.)

Once downloaded, open the QR reader and point the camera on your phone at the QR code in the book.

The app will then ask you to open the linked webpage in a browser.

Once the webpage has opened, you'll see ... well, I'll let that be a surprise.

If you're reading this as an eBook, simply tap the QR code to go to the web page.

INTRODUCTION

This isn't a book written from a mountaintop. It hasn't come off the heels of some life-changing moment. I haven't just been given some honorary theological doctorate, won an acting award, had a song or album "go platinum," or started raising my first child and just happened upon all this new-found wisdom that HAD to be written down.

This is a good time to make sure we're all on the same page, literally. If I can, I'd just like to go ahead and establish a definition for the term, *Christianese*. This term may be new to you or as familiar as that one friend who just lets themselves into your house without knocking. Christianese words tend to use a lot of weather and topography-oriented metaphors. For instance, let's talk about the good ole phrase, "spiritual mountaintop." I define a mountaintop as any good moment in life where you may feel recently accomplished, newly encouraged, in the middle of an exciting and needed change, or possibly just sensing relief for the first time in a while. Christians love mountaintop seasons. This last sentence is a li'l two-for because it incorporates both weather (seasons) AND topography (mountaintop). I would have gotten bonus points for that combo on any game show. Any. Game. Show. Ever.

Spiritual mountaintops are "loved moments" for us because they're usually times when we're seeing breakthroughs and the harvest of hard work or diligence, enjoying some rest, or just feeling especially good about what God is doing in our lives. It's that time in our walk with Jesus, however brief or extended it may be, where we feel new, able to take a deep breath, notice a sunset, or just enjoy a moment we hadn't before.

I admit I did not write this book from a mountaintop because I don't want to imply I'm writing completely on the other side of my struggle. Many self-help books are written with the perspective of, "I used to really struggle with 'this thing,' but now I don't. Let's applaud me for how I did it." Although there are many phenomenal authors and brilliant thought-leaders in the world today, I find there to be a bit of lack when it comes to honesty about the full story. There is a lack on the side of communicating the journey and declaring what's true in the middle of the journey. What does it look like to be in the middle of the lowest valley in your life and still choose rightly? What does it look like to read and understand someone's completely messy and thrown-together life as they themselves, in this scenario, myself, begin to understand it?

I have a great deal of respect for those who can sit on the victorious side of a great battle and feel no need to explain their fight. In the same way, I also have a great deal of respect for someone who experiences a victory and can, with accuracy and intention, teach others how to have that victory for themselves. However, the authors I connect with and learn the most from are the ones who are vulnerable and open. Reading a book about how someone else used to have a, b, or c problem and how they "suddenly saw the light" and are writing to show how you can too is about as low on my to-do list as learning the lyrics to any Jewel song. And if you're just a big ole Jewel fan, look up the duet by Jessica Simpson and Jewel online and be blessed.

This book is going to be a whirlwind of stories, thoughts, jokes, beliefs, heartaches, victories, and struggles. How they all intertwine will help you understand a perfectly-in-process me. This book is going to include snapshots from my lowest "valleys" (Christianese for *low moments in life*) to my highest mountaintops. However, the earnest intention of my heart is not to spend time showing you some great victory in my life for which I need your affirmation. Nor is it my intent to walk you to the banks of my lowest moment to elicit your pity or empathy. My intention in writing this book is to walk you into, possibly for the first time, intimacy with the God I find marvelous. I can't help but communicate and bring you into my story because I love to share what I love with those I love. And I know it may seem like pandering or some sort of false investment, but I truly love the reader for whom I wrote this book. Hint: if you're reading this page, you are the reader I love.

I've never cared a great deal for face value relationships or flippant and meaningless friendships. I do life with those I love with an intensity that has pushed away a few, but that has led me to have some of the most meaningful friendships I've known. I'm quite vocal about how much I love relationship, so I'd be a liar and a fraud if I wasn't obedient to the Lord to write this book for you. If my love doesn't call me into obedience and action, then it is not true love. That's a little something I learned from watching Jesus obey His Father, even to the point of His own death. Christ's obedience compelled me to write, but did that motivation stop me from dragging and kicking my feet into obedience? Why no, no it didn't. Still, God has a way of taking our little "yeses" and accomplishing mighty things with them. So, my prayer is that the following pages will meet you where you're at, make you feel seen and known, loved and championed. More than anything, I want you to be challenged and jump-started into your true God-given identity and purpose. So, without further ado, let us begin.

FIRST: HONESTY

1

In no way have I ever desired to write a book.

In truth, I have sneered at several nonfiction books written by people my age. This aversion is not because I don't believe in their ability as writers and world changers but because there's something discrediting to me about a young person sharing their thoughts and asking anyone to take them seriously; it's somewhat confusing since I'm a young person writing a book, but hang in there, and I'll explain what I mean.

This is as good a place to start as any.

I've been concerned with the "credibility" of people my whole life. It hasn't been that I look for and expect someone to have a doctorate degree or years of ministry experience before I listen to what they have to say. But I've always had to have respect for a person before I respected their thoughts. I needed to feel loved before I could be corrected. When I smelled a whiff of ulterior motive, I would shut down and become quite spiteful. I've run the gamut of stereotypical reactions to correction for which Millennials are famous. I'm not saying it's great, but it's the truth.

So, if you're reading this first chapter waiting to shoot down my thoughts as idyllic, immature, or, even worse, "millennial," just know that I get it. I often want to shoot down my own thoughts and ideas because I know the deep darkness I've fought and with which I still contend. I know the battles of will and faith I've won, and, in doing so,

I've seen God do miraculous things. But I've also lost a good number of battles. I've yielded to sin patterns and lies; some have bullied me into a corner and others I've welcomed with open arms. I have proudly boasted about the work of Christ in my life while quietly asking God if He even cares. I have walked through seasons of defeat that felt like an unending barrage of daggers to the heart. But God continues to uphold me and bring me higher; so, what am I going to do? Staying silent is no longer an option.

I am in no way on the other side. In fact, I'm still in the throes of life, choosing daily to yield and submit my heart to Christ. So, from one in-process person to another, let me say, *It's okay.* God's not bothered by my tenure as a believer. He's glad I'm willing to speak. I've learned He is a huge fan of matching honesty and vulnerability with His power. Turns out, I'm a big fan of it, too.

On paper, it doesn't make sense. But welcome to the Kingdom of God where the weakest are made strong in Him and where what makes sense on paper doesn't always matter to God. Our sense and what we think is correct is an incomplete picture of the full story.

Culture has taught us to be paralyzed by our own weakness, to stand still in it. We're told to wallow in our hurts and the self-serving emotions that become our confidants. Frankly, I'm exhausted with the amount of garbage thinking that's being shoved down my generation's throat. It's killing us, and the Church, for the most part, has been quite content to make the issue ours. I am not meaning to incite some kind of blame war. As for the condition of the Millennial generation and world, the blame is ours. All ours.

Let's start with something that seems incredibly difficult for a lot of Christians to digest. The standard and truth of the Word has not changed, but the culture, which serves as a soundtrack to our thoughts and beliefs, has. Truth has remained the same, while biases, wounds, opinions, fallacies, evil, and plain ole ignorance have built an ugly idol to try and obscure our view of actual truth.

See, the message of present day culture is confusing. You're told to be accepting of everyone ... unless they think differently than you. In that case, assert your claims in a way that condescends and belittles those who hold an opposing view. In fact, if you have a college degree, be sure to make anyone who has an unpopular thought feel like an idiot. That way you feel superior, and people think you're smart.

We're told to love, and that love comes in all shapes and forms ... but when love becomes inconvenient or requires more of us than we want to give, we can just bail. We're told not to offend anyone's feelings; however, if we feel offended, we have the right to wage full scale war. We're told our behaviors, the way we dress and how we talk, are who we are. So, we focus on the outside, champion and demean it all at once, and wonder why we're not functioning correctly.

We're told in nearly every TV show and movie that true love looks like a carefully coordinated love scene; forget loving someone more than you do your own sexual desires or honoring their body and heart. That would almost be too much. Why would I play the long game of working to gain real, lasting intimacy with a person when I could choose the empty replica of intimacy in casual sex? After all, having sex is easy. Having intimacy is hard work. We're told our bad habits are quirks. Our desires and appetites are natural and not to be governed. In fact, if you do govern your desires or abstain from sex outside of a committed marriage, you're made to look and feel like an out-of-touch prude who can't accept reality. Sin and misery love company. I don't know if you've noticed, but the world is not currently increasing in love. It's increasing in brokenness.

Confused by this? If so, no worries. Check out page 8!

We're told to focus on "truth" but to mostly focus on "my truth." This lie that is peddled, bought, and sold cheaply is the most damaging. It tells us that we get to live in our own bubble with decisions that only impact us, that we can create our own subjective moral compass and standard by which to live. Oh, and if anyone else's truth crosses our truth, we should immediately retreat to "my truth." We're taught, because it's mine, it must be right for me (insert eye roll here).

We're told not to believe in and submit to God because we must never actually look or appear as though we need someone bigger than ourselves. But don't worry, if you want to self-justify and still look like a Christian, you're completely good and clear to pull out the occasional verse or theological principle, strip it from its true context, and serve it up separate from the rest of the Word that empowers that very principle.

Culture has reduced relationship with the Lord to, "I believe in a *Higher Power.*"

It's so convenient. You see, you don't have to *obey* a "Higher Power." And a Higher Power isn't going to require too much of you. Culture paints an image of the Lord that holds Him solely responsible for the evil in the world but gives Him no credit for the good. How many times have you heard the question, "Well if God's so good, then why would He let _____ happen?" It's not even worth giving a specific example because I'm sure you've already got a few in your mind. No one needs help being mad at God, whether they believe in Him or not.

If possible, I would set that whole "my truth" pile of thinking and the lies that empower it on fire. I guess I should tell you ... I'm a little passionate. So, you'll excuse me if I say, gently and with the utmost respect, back off my generation. We're working through a few things, okay?

We've inherited, as young people, an untended garden of belief systems for which we've been made to feel solely responsible. I do not in any way excuse our role in believing the lies that have been spoon-fed to our generation. We're told at many points we're entitled, self-serving, unaware, inconsiderate, disrespectful, and rebellious; yet, we're responding to the very environment that has fostered us and the labels assigned to us. Unhealed brokenness begets brokenness.

We inherited brokenness, and, because of the exponential rate at which culture has grown in unhealth, we are now at a point when the line between truth and lies has melded in the hearts of most people, becoming impossible to differentiate. Our brokenness, and the emotions that acknowledge it, force their way to the surface by way of rebellion, acting out, and grandstanding.

Maybe this acting out is rooted in the fact that we've wanted our wounds dressed and our brokenness correctly set in love AND truth. Maybe, just maybe, our perceived rebellion has been a response to form without function, rules without actual love, healing that's topical rather than deep enough to reach the actual wound. We've been told to toughen up and move on, but we're spiritual babies who need the

Church to be more than it has been. We need the Church to leave the four walls of comfortable thinking and recycled programs. We need Christians to get down on the ground with Jesus as He meets us where we're at to then pull us higher.

We've been left to our own devices, and our own devices are killing us.

So, this is the choice at hand: as a younger generation, we can either sit around griping about the mess of our hurts and how we've felt abandoned and spiritually left to fend for ourselves, or we can get up and recognize that the decision to grow and pursue wholeness in Christ is ours. Deep down, we all know there's something about His Name. Even now, as you're reading this paragraph, regardless of your age, my prayer is that you would be made acutely aware of Jesus' presence.

I've spent a lot of time trying to love people at all walks of life because, to be honest, relationship is about the most fulfilling thing to me on earth. You know something I've found common in the atheist and the devout believer? They both need Jesus. And, if it's difficult for you to stomach Jesus as the Healer, Provider, Joy-giver, Sustainer, Fulfiller of Promises, and Hope itself ... that's okay. He's not bothered.

I'm not bothered. In fact, it's just one more place where He gets to reveal His goodness. As you press past the comfortable places in your mind into the unknown, or even further, into the areas you've tried to shut down and off, you will see that your eyes will begin to clear. You will become stronger than you thought possible. And it will all be because of Christ. Whether you choose to give Him your heart, pursue deeper relationship, or to walk away from faith altogether, He will remain patient and loving. His love is not landlocked or stopped by your response.

Now, we are not talking about heaven or hell here. We're talking about the fact that Jesus loves to love on us, whether we ever choose Him back. That's His nature and innate character. However, I need to be responsible in saying that eternity in heaven is only promised for those who choose Him. As anyone who desires genuine relationship, Jesus is not trying to manipulate you into choosing Him. He loves us purely and wholly, and our response to that love results in either life or death.

Throughout this book, I'll refer to "the enemy" a few times. I don't want anyone to be confused about who I mean when you see this phrase. The enemy is Satan. In Genesis 3, he tempted Adam and Eve to doubt God's goodness. He's been doing the same thing ever since. Satan doesn't want anyone to see or know Jesus, so he tempts people to believe that having created things is better than a relationship with their Creator. Along with tempting, Satan is also the accuser. He reminds people of their failures and the labels that others incorrectly place on them. He desires people to accept hopelessness and brokenness as their identity and worldview. The only language Satan speaks: lies. He tempts, accuses, and lies with the purpose of stealing, killing, and destroying a person's soul. He does this not because people are important to him; rather, he works to destroy people because people are important to God. Satan is not the equal of Jesus in any way, despite how he's portrayed in a few horror movies. He's not Jesus, God in human flesh. Jesus came to the earth to destroy the works of Satan. So, when the enemy accuses me, Jesus stands as my Advocate who cancels out the power of all accusations and condemnations against me. When Satan tempts or accuses me, Jesus says, "Cavanaugh, no matter how you feel or what you're tempted to pursue right now, you are Mine, and I love you. I'm the Truth who defines you." Remember, I promised you honesty.

Now, if you're breathing, you've probably heard "honesty" used in a litany of ways that almost always ends up hurting someone ... cough ... you. Often, those who champion their willingness to hurt your feelings do so behind the bulletproof glass of, "I'm just being honest." The issue is that we've learned to use honesty as a Trojan Horse for letting out personal, or at times completely unrelated, frustration or hurt. We add some sarcasm and a "gotcha" face and hope that the person receiving our dagger-like words is immune to feeling the very hurt with which we're trying to cope. In turn, we learn to associate honesty with hurt and a lack of actual care or love. We have made honesty the enemy and our own hurts the reason for avoiding it at all costs. So, we repeat an unhealthy cycle, never being fully honest because we've seen the damage it does in the hands of those who care more about sharing their hurt than healing it.

Just so we're clear, I have and do fall into that category at times, even though it's not my heart's intent. I've learned that, if I let it, the voice of personal hurt will always be louder than what my heart is trying to communicate. Those are the moments where I have to remind myself: If my honesty with a friend, family member, co-worker, or person on the street leaves them feeling uncared for and uncovered, I have missed the mark.

The purpose of complete honesty is not to take advantage of a vulnerable heart, but to heal it. Honesty should be used to bring clarity and understanding to a situation, behavior, or thought process. I hinted at this earlier, but brokenness that is only set in truth and not love does more damage than leaving a wound undressed.

Lord, I thank You for whoever
is reading this book right now.
I know You are a God who honors
our willingness to ask hard questions
and hear hard truths. So, as these
chapters unfold, I ask that You
shield the reader's heart from offense
or the need to self-defend. I ask
that You reveal Your heart and
that Your love would be the
aroma on every page.

THE HARD CHAPTER

2

"So much time and so little to do. Wait a minute. Strike that. Reverse it." – Willy Wonka

To be honest, Willy Wonka has never felt more apropos. There's a great deal I want to share, and I realize for it to carry the weight I'm praying it will carry, a foundation must be laid. Now, if your introduction to me has been through Instagram, you may know me as a high-energy, almost nauseatingly loud, and intense personality trying to crack as many jokes as possible in one minute.

As much as I do love making people laugh and being a source of joy in that way, I want to reveal my heart and mind to you. So, if you'll allow me, I'd like to give you some background, so we have a solid place to begin our journey together. You need to know a bit of my story to help you trust me; so, this is basically my attempt at establishing some ethos.

I'm the youngest of four siblings; there's no real surprise there. I grew up in the heart of the Dallas/Fort Worth area of Texas. I am quite fortunate to have two of the most kind, God-fearing, loving, brilliant, and generous parents this world has known. I have two older brothers and a sister and am separated in age from them by four, six, and seven years, but they have loved me well, regardless. I'll break down a few of the strengths and characteristics I see in my own family members, and then we'll see how I fit into the puzzle.

My father: My father has an incredibly brilliant, bottom-line, focused mind. He's also quite sensitive to truth and is a leader of leaders. He is patient and treats my mother with so much respect and dignity. He's truly shown us what it looks like to love someone more than yourself. He is also about as well-respected as they come and has always wielded a certain amount of healthy fear in every office or boardroom he enters. My father is a very successful businessman and has been running companies since he was in his young 20s. The amount of respect I have for him is unparalleled.

My mother: My mother is as kind, thorough, and intentional as they come. She loves her husband, children, and nine grandchildren with a selflessness I don't know that I've seen elsewhere. If there were honorary doctorates given for hospitality and the understanding of etiquette, my mother would be a fast contender. Also, she throws down in the kitchen. I mean, Martha Stewart wishes she had half the class of my mother is what I'm saying.

My oldest brother: My brother is incredibly sensitive and such a strong leader. He is exceptional in business as well as being one of the most thorough outdoorsmen you'll ever meet. To top it all off, he is a phenomenal golfer and has always loved sports and most everything that is stereotypically male. So, it would only make sense God would give him four beautiful little girls. He is the best father to them and loves them so well.

My sister: My sister inherited my father's practical thinking and way of communicating. She doesn't suffer fools which is something I admire about her. She has two of the sweetest and kindest children, who absolutely adore her. She's an exceptional mother. She has a heart that sees a need and ways to remedy that need unlike I've seen in others. She is justice-minded, focused, and makes a great ally for anyone.

My older brother: My brother is one of the smartest people I know. He is a lawyer and outstanding golfer. Because he's that talented, he can just do both. He is easy to be around and is always willing to banter with the best of them, so he obviously makes for a great sparring partner. He shares in my father and brother's love of the outdoors and is one of the best marksmen I know. He's got three lovely and precious children that I adore and who wholly love their daddy.

I'm honored to be in this lineage and to round out this amazing team of players. I wish I could say that I always felt this way about my family, but, unfortunately, I didn't. In fact, I spent a great deal of my childhood trying to understand how I belonged in this family. It wasn't because I didn't think they were amazing. It was because I felt out of place from as early as I can remember.

I'm not sure my parents were ever fully aware that taking me to see *Cats* at age three would light a creative fire in me. The story goes that they sat me down in the seat and immediately felt the glares of fellow theatregoers concerned about sitting so close to a child in the theatre.

Once the lights went down and the overture started, I was transfixed and remained so until intermission. The people nearby were apparently shocked and impressed by how "adult" I was in my theatre viewing. I'd love to say I've gotten less intense about loving theatre, but that would be a lie. From that moment at *Cats*, I was immediately hooked on the arts and creativity.

As a child, I was an awful lot to deal with, I'm sure. I was incredibly passionate, some would say "obsessive," about anything I loved. Adding to my zeal for theatre, I have always had a high timbered voice, demonstrative gestures, and animated expressions. Well, it doesn't take a rocket scientist to guess where this is going.

I mean, can we level with each other? We can pretend that stereotypes don't exist and that we don't size up people by what we see, but that wouldn't be honest. As soon as I realized I was artistic and started to express my creativity as a young person, it didn't take long for the labels and cautious conversations about my sexuality to surface. Almost as a preventative measure to correct the perceived issue at hand, I was over-introduced to outdoor activities and sports.

I saw as my brothers grew up that they had a slew of influential men who wanted to pour into them by including them in weekly rounds of golf along with regular hunting trips. I began to see the ever-growing gap between the way my brothers were loved and the way I was loved. My parents did their absolute best in dealing with their creative son, but I know it wasn't easy for them. The truth was they didn't have a blueprint for me. I was so different from my siblings that I think a great deal of time was spent trying to understand me. I don't blame them because I was trying to understand myself. I was trying to understand why I constantly felt out of place. I was trying to understand why I had an innate feeling of dirtiness. I was trying to understand why I couldn't really connect with many of the kids my age. And, because I am about equal parts "feeler" as I am analytical "thinker," I constantly felt like I was in between reason and emotion, and my emotions usually got the better of me. So, I was a high-strung, easily upset boy who didn't respond to correction well and skeptically viewed everyone in my life.

Before we dive into what I inevitably ended up believing about my family and my identity, it's important to share one of my first memories. My parents had a few babysitters they used on a regular basis. When I was between four and six years old, we had a babysitter with long hair who I really loved. Now obviously her beautiful hair wasn't the only reason I loved her. She was an awesome babysitter. But I had a real affinity for babysitters with incredibly long hair and a bit of a crush on this specific one. In fact, I would blush and immediately become embarrassed whenever my parents would call attention to it, as they often enjoyed doing. I remember the day I learned she had married and cut her hair. You would've thought someone killed my dog. We're talking that level of deep mourning.

As we delve into what I believed about my identity and what was and has continued to be spoken over me for 20 plus years, I want us to remember my first crush was on a girl named Wendy. That is irrefutable. Nothing the devil could try to convince me of changes that fact. Truthfully, he hates that he can't erase this memory from me, and he would love nothing more than to do that.

I don't believe in burying the lead, so I want to be quite clear as to what I intend to communicate. The devil works to separate and isolate us from the truth by putting distance between the truth and our memories. He coerces us into choosing sin by changing our perspective. He reminds us of the labels others use to verbally identify us, and he works to give those spoken labels tangible power to become our "new" identities. He binds and shackles us by using our little, and seemingly subtle, mental agreements with his suggested thoughts. Then he carries us down gradual paths that slowly change from light-filled open fields to claustrophobic and terrifying forests. This is what it looks like when we believe lies about ourselves; I know this from experience.

The first time I remember being called gay was in 4th grade. However, from the time I was four, I can remember being told by different leaders in church, my own family members, teachers, and coaches that I acted like a girl. From my mannerisms, to the way I spoke, to how I told a story, to the songs I liked singing, to how I walked, I was made to believe that there was something wrong with me.

I don't blame any person in my life for not knowing what to do or think about me, but the truth is I became accustomed and used to a real and tangible loneliness. I felt as though, before I walked into any classroom, I had to brace myself for comments from the boys. I would think of a slew of insults to hurl if backed into a corner. I learned early on that my survival in school was going to have to come from my wit and using it as a weapon. Because of that, I became wildly defensive and was quick to put everyone else down before they had the chance to do the same to me. It was a horrible way of existing, but it was what I learned to do to survive.

Since I already felt as though I was a black sheep, I started leaning into the darkness that had been spoken over me. I began to believe, wholeheartedly, what a great deal of others already thought about me. That was when my slow and gradual descent to rock bottom began. I'm glad now that it did begin because it led me to a place of desperation. I was either going to choose the God who had been knocking on the door of my heart since I was born or lean into how I wanted to live and resolve myself to never submit to God because of an inaccurate identity first spoken over me. After years of not understanding what my voice and gestures had to do with my sexuality, I finally gave in to the barrage of voices that had been trying to define me for so long.

As I'm sure you've experienced, there is a certain way we address the things people say about us. If it's something out of left field that doesn't even compute in our minds and has no basis, we can easily dismiss it saying, "Well, that's ridiculous." If it's something that we have heard before, we may give it a little more attention, but in the end resolve ourselves to the fact, "They just don't get it, and that's okay." Then there are those few choice daggers, the ones that play on the internal monologue you've already been hearing, the ones that back up something someone else said, the ones that hurt more than the rest.

My dagger has always been my sexuality. It's been an area where I have had to fight to believe rightly about myself for the entirety of my life. If this is an area in which you've contended, I'm not here to excuse or to empower the lie that God creates us with sexual cravings that He specifically warns us in Scripture not to engage in because of their harmfulness. This isn't even an area of argument, and it burdens my heart that so many Christian leaders have taken to trying to find allowance for homosexuality in Scripture as opposed to trying to see the loving caution to abstain from this lifestyle or activity. And quickly, I don't believe homosexuality is unpardonable. I do not believe God loves those who practice it any less. I believe God has amazing stories of redemption for each person who chooses Jesus, and I don't believe it is my job to cast any bit of condemnation on the walk of another person. So, if you're reading this book, living in the gay lifestyle and thinking I'm about to condemn you, I assure you that is not what is happening. Your heart is safe with me.

I'm offering up my own story to encourage you. My hope is that, in hearing about how I fought (and continue to fight) for my own freedom in Christ, you might experience freedom, too. Also, if you're someone reading this with cynical eyes, believing, *Bless his heart ... he just doesn't know that he's gay, made that way, and can't accept it,* I would gently like to ask you to refrain from condescension and from excusing my beliefs as naivety until the end of this book. I assure you that my beliefs have been developed from an honest and real place, and that my encounters with and revelation from the Lord have been out of an earnest desire to understand and live the way I'm intended.

You may sense a little sharpness in my tone, but I promise its intent is not for the reader, but for the very real enemy I know is at work to distract and discredit the Truth. I have found myself in conversations with so many older, gay men who think they're going to be the ones to escort me out of the closet into "my true self." As well-meaning as they may or may not have been, it's just not an area in my life the devil gets ground in anymore. I know who I am, and it doesn't matter how I come across or how high I can sing or how "sassy" someone thinks I am. I'm not moved anymore. Also, maybe just stop calling guys "sassy." There are few words more emasculating than that. I'm only recently getting to the place where I no longer feel the need to defend myself in this area. So, I'd ask for a little grace as we both see the grip in my hands loosen throughout this chapter. I promise it will. I know so many others who have contended for their identity in this area, and, like many of them, I too have been uncovered and condemned more times than I care to count. Be that as it may, I will not continue that cycle. Despite being wounded by well-meaning but poor-functioning Christians, I continue to believe God's heart is to restore dignity and honor to all people who are created in His image and whom He loves. Bullies may have stripped us of honor, but God speaks over us an honorable, irrevocable identity.

I'm now in a place in my life where I can look at this sin and its own effect in my life as no different as any other, meaning that it's all quite harmful. I haven't always believed that. I think it's important to give some context for those of you who are reading this who may have never struggled in this area. Those who have a relationship with or knowledge of God who are same-sex attracted, usually feel condemned, isolated, wrong, and dirty. That is the base level of what someone dealing with this temptation believes. A lot of people who have never experienced same-sex attraction will say that "it's a choice" or that it's something people decide to be. These people are ignorant, for lack of a stronger word. Although the decision to engage with the sin remains in the hands of the person experiencing the temptation, I will assure you that not one person who has struggled with this sin can tell you when they "decided" to be gay. That is the first line of thinking that the Church needs to drop, pronto.

The way that my relationship with this sin began was first by the word curses spoken over me like, "That looks gay," "Don't do that; you look like a girl," to high school, when I was called a "fag" the first day of freshman year. I hate that word and don't mean to offend, but I think it's important to paint an accurate and real picture so that we can be on the same page. From the first time you hear it about yourself, whether knowingly or unknowingly, it's easy to start toying with the idea. You ask yourself questions like, *What did I do that communicated that? Why would they think that about me?* Then a few more times of hearing it about yourself, and it's no longer possible to differentiate what you've been told by others from what you believe about yourself. It then grows to where you feel as though, when you walk into a room, you carry the aroma of what's been spoken over you without even getting the chance to say, "No, wait. I know I come across this way, but I'm actually not." Any attempt to tell someone their read on you is wrong is met with an eye roll and an, "Okay sure, queer." Today, if you say someone's assessment of you is wrong, you're simply made to feel like a liar, someone who hasn't come to terms with it, someone who is repressing it, or someone who is self-loathing altogether. It makes it nearly impossible to see any solid truth because your very identity isn't believed when you communicate it. At least that was the case for me.

Then there is the barrage of coaches and sports players in high school who make it their mission to emasculate you. Or was that just me? See, that is all run-of-the-mill for those who have contended in this area. It's not something that's this sweet and empowering *Lifetime* movie about just always knowing it about yourself and finally having this self-accepting moment. The devil assigns demons to accomplish their work long before sexual desire even enters the picture. The Lord uses all things for our good, but the devil uses all curses to our detriment. I am in no way meaning to depress you or apply some sort of guilt. I want to give you an accurate picture. There are only so many times you can be called "fat" before you start to believe you are fat.

There are only so many times someone can call you "ugly" before you believe it. There are only so many times someone can reject you before you start to believe you're worthy of rejection. And there are only so many times you can be told you're "gay" before you start to agree with the label. Now, I realize this isn't the same pathway that every person in this area walks down, but it is mine.

I remember wanting a girlfriend in the 5th grade; genuinely having a crush on a girl and getting butterflies and all the things that accompany a crush. Then recess would come, and I wouldn't be the first one picked. I wasn't great in really any sport we played, and so the guys my age and my coach, a grown man, would make a couple of derogatory comments in front of my crush. Laughing would ensue, and I would be devastated.

Outside the Church, bullying against people who struggle with homosexual temptation still exists regardless of the way homosexuality is popularly portrayed today and how culture has decided to view it positively. But someone struggling with this temptation inside the Church often feels like they can't be open about their struggle because of a stigma attached to this issue. In many unspoken ways, they feel especially dirty in the company of Christians. I promised you honesty, and I'm doing my part. So, meet me in the middle. I will speak the truth and do so without fear of repercussion or of making anyone mad because I believe so firmly in the harmfulness of this specific sin. I'm willing to be hated for speaking on this specific subject if just one person finds freedom through my honesty. I've been given the Word of God, Truth

Himself, the Holy Spirit, and decades of looking straight on at this issue of identity and the death homosexuality brings. I've seen it rip and tear away at my own life and peace. I'm not here for it, nor will I stand idly by and applaud death while celebrating it as "freedom" in others.

That's a lie.

My generation is far more aware of the spiritual realm than most people would like to acknowledge. To acknowledge and give voice to what you know in the most central part of your being brings about accountability. When accountability comes into play, then there is a belief in an absolute right and an absolute wrong. When there's an absolute right or wrong, then we're required to be responsible for that information and how we handle it. Since my generation has been taught that accountability and an absolute right and wrong come with condemnation and rules, we run from the reality of absolute truth. Instead, we stay in ambiguity and tell each other: "Whatever you think is best." "Well, if that's right for you." "Ya know, I could see how you'd think that. If that's your truth, man, go for it."

We have silently and, at times, loudly cheered our brothers and sisters on as they walk into more and more sin that brings more and more death. But because we haven't submitted our wills, thoughts, hearts, and ideals to the One greater than ourselves, we become our own gods. And just to clue you in, we make terrible gods. We make powerless, weak, incomplete, hurt, reactionary, and empty gods ... unable to distinguish sin from truth, light from darkness, and unable to recognize who God created us to be from whom we've distorted by our selfishness.

We then create more fractured and hurt people who are surrounded by no sign of parameter, no truth, and no actual love. Without the loving boundaries set by the One who is the absolute Truth, we have no power to be more than we've always been told we are by others or ourselves.

There have been ministries that claimed they had the ability to rehabilitate and recalibrate sexual desire only to then be publicly annihilated when founders or recipients of their ministry fell back into sin. Yes, into sin. Sorry, you're not going to hear me mince words with this one. You can bring whatever study you want to the table, whatever biblical commentary, whatever verses you have dissected to squeeze support for your belief, and I will not move from that stance. Homosexuality has never been a part of God's design for human flourishing, or even something He encourages us to pursue.

I'd like to just go ahead and state that being open about my belief on homosexuality is not easy for me. In fact, this is probably one of the scarier things I've done in my life. I've not been incredibly open about my thoughts on same-sex attraction or even my own story in general because I've never fully felt on the other side of it or that I've got this thing figured out. I know how sin is, and I know that, left to my own devices, I'm as close to believing a lie as I am to walking in the Light. That's the nature of a relationship with the Lord. My dependence on Him doesn't then lead me to independence, where I have it all together. My daily dependence on God reminds me of how dependent I am on Him. I'm not one of those people who can just pop in church every now and then and keep on keeping on. If I'm not spending time every single day with the Lord, I am quickly reminded why casual faith isn't an option for me. I need Jesus. And I need Jesus to be Jesus to me every day.

What I'm seeing is that my dependence on the Lord establishes a deeper root system in me, so I can stand and not be subjected to how I feel. I love a metaphor, so go with me here. I imagine us like trees, and our faith/relationship with God is like an extensive root system. I've lived enough life trying to hold on during storms of intense emotions, depression, loneliness, and circumstances with roots that only go a few inches into the ground. You know what I've found? The storm usually wins. So, what I do to withstand and thrive in the middle of a torrential downpour is to go deep with the Lord. If I am not deeply dependent on Him and His Word, it is game over for me the second the wind changes. I know me and the ways the devil comes at me. Even knowing myself and the enemy's ways doesn't keep me from saying "no" to the sin if I haven't stayed connected to the Lord.

This issue of homosexuality is such a dividing force in the Church, in the world, and in the hearts and minds of those contending with it. Let's start there. It's a polarizing subject and one veered away from at all costs by most leaders in the Christian community. Now, you may be thinking of a sermon you once heard or a leader you know who has a thorough understanding of this subject. Those people and their hearts are amazing. However, such thoughtful Christians, specifically around the subject of homosexuality, are largely outliers.

The typical response in the Church to a person who deals with this temptation makes the struggling person feel depraved, dirty, broken, unfixable, or worse, abandoned altogether. Out of fear, we as the Church have left those tormented by this sin to fend for themselves. When Christians try to help people dealing with same-sex attraction, they can become angry when their efforts to help prove futile. We have emphasized the weight of sin as opposed to the weight and gravity of authentic relationship with Christ. We have taught, not in word but in action, that the sin of homosexuality carries more weight and a graver punishment when the Word clearly applies the same penalty to all sin: death. This means that the time you lied to your parents about where you were going ... yeah, that sin carries the same penalty as the most perverse sin you can imagine in the eyes of God. So, let's just level the playing field here if possible.

The Church has oversimplified this area and made little effort in understanding people who deal with homosexual temptations. We who have struggled in this area have felt the condescension, judgment, and uncovering from the very leadership who are in place to love and protect us and point us to the cross. We have been made to feel as though we've made some conscious decision to choose one attraction over the other. We have been shown how dealing with this temptation separates us from our community, our families, and from serving the Lord. We have been put down and brought low in the process. We've been told about the severity of our sin but given little guidance to walk through and out of it. We've been made to think that any sexual temptation starts out as a blatant attempt to choose our way over God's way, and yet most of us who have struggled in this area have done so most of our lives, as far back as early childhood. We have been assigned and given irredeemable labels that act like cement blocks on our feet. As we stand stuck, those whose sin conditions are more interior lightly walk by and look with haughty pity on those who are "best left to work out *that* thing on their own." Just for a little bonus, the first of the seven things God detests the most is "haughty eyes."[1] I wonder what would happen if we spent just a little more time focusing on our own arrogance and superiority than we do putting down those who are contending with mental and spiritual battles. Or maybe even, who knows, we could love people where they're at and let Jesus do the rest.

We teach by the way we live, love, or don't love our neighbor. We accept the false idea that right doing leads to right thinking and that right thinking leads to right belief. Now I want to be clear, I know a great many people come to know the Lord before major changes happen. Some people, before they are even introduced to Christ, immediately know and tell themselves, "I have to stop sleeping around." So they stop sleeping around, and this action brings healthy fruit and growth in their lives. That's not everyone's story. Some people believe the truth before they change, and some people change before they believe the truth. To lump both groups together would be dangerous. By design, our right beliefs will lead to right thinking which will lead to right doing. When we try to prescribe those steps out of order in the area of sexuality, we've already lost. We have prescribed a topical treatment of "do and live right" without first addressing the initial core belief about one's identity. The most fundamental part of us is who we believe God to be and who we believe ourselves to be. You can build the most beautiful and luxurious home possible, but if that foundation is already cracked and fragmented before you put the framework up, good luck. A person lives without a sense of grounded identity if they don't answer these two identity questions: one, *Who do I know God to be?* and, two, *Who do I know myself to be?*

Culture hasn't helped us at all in answering these identity questions. It tells us that masculinity looks like a love for the outdoors, an affinity for sports, a willingness and ability to fight, and a collection of proud sexual escapades. Society says masculinity is measured by how much money a man can amass, the power he has in any given job, the way he is perceived when walking into a room, and the list goes on and on. The problem is, the way the Church defines masculinity and the way the world defines it have bled together. Church conferences around the country are themed to the gills with all things "masculine," using a definition of the term never given by God. This masculine theme is paired with a bunch of pastors telling good ole boy jokes that isolate, condescend, and speak down to creative types and young people altogether. I've personally been to a number of meetings where pastors put down the way men on the worship team dress, the way they do their hair, the songs they sing, and the music they like. The audience laughs and laughs, and you'll look around to find that it's mostly older men getting a laugh at the expense of creative types. Maybe this is an area to look at when discussing dwindling Church numbers and the reason why so many churches are struggling to keep Millennials in the door. Just maybe.

If you're reading this chapter and find yourself already angry or in disagreement with my thoughts, that's okay. Being offended is a choice, and, if this is hard for you to stomach, perhaps you're being called to walk upstream. The question now is, are you going to go with the current or stand up and start to walk? This chapter isn't written for the dead branch that wants to stay dead and unbothered as it floats to the mouth of a waterfall. I'm tired of walking with, talking to, and trying to carry dead branches that profess their liveliness.

A Christian man with sexual desires for the opposite sex grows up knowing in the back of his mind that he will most likely find love, get married, have children, and that his parents will be excited about it. Even as I write this, I'm struggling to find the right words to say what I'm meaning to communicate and nothing more. In earlier drafts of this chapter, I made a claim that those who don't struggle with same-sex attraction automatically grow up with one less thing with which to deal. Now, upon further examination, I realize that my assumption is not true. We all struggle differently and live in a variety of circumstances. I have no substantiated support to make the claim that those who don't struggle with same-sex attraction have somewhat easier lives. Obviously, that is not verbatim what I said, but it is absolutely the inference I made.

I think this perspective comes from a place of suffering. I grew up feeling halted from my very purpose and true identity based off of my own sexual cravings. It seemed as though everyone around me was able to move forward and upward with their lives, while I was left at the starting line, asking the question, *Well, if I can't even sort out why I'm attracted to who I'm attracted to and figure this thing out, how am I going to be able to do anything productive with my life?* I know this sounds bleak, but it's really valuable to understand the reality of those who have chosen Jesus and yet still deal with very real and tangible temptation. The fight to believe and live in truth that is completely counter to everything we feel is no joke, and it's not for the weak. But is it for *"the weak made strong"*[2] in Him? Absolutely.

The sins and issues that are given the most attention are the more salacious, shocking, or outwardly deplorable ones as opposed to the more seemingly mute, placid, or harmless. Obviously, there's no such thing as a harmless sin, but we're currently talking about the way we view things, not the way things actually are. There is an attitude pervading in Church culture that lessens the destructiveness of inward sin in exchange for the witch hunt one can have searching for the sins more easily seen. Don't believe me? How about this: if you worked at a church or grew up in one, you may have noticed that those who most often got "let go" or "sat down" from ministry were dismissed because of sexual sin that was made public. Now I understand this reason for dismissal 100%; but why are we not as quick to deal with manipulation, gossip, legalism, rudeness, and arrogance, for starters? Why are we more prone to crucify those whose sin seems more tangible? I'll tell you why: the battleground of sexuality is one the enemy would love to keep control of, and the best way he can do that is to get God's people to serve his self-righteous, bullying agenda. If the devil can convince you that calling out someone's sin to shame them is somehow your duty, then he's won real ground. Of course, the devil would never let you know that strategy. But the second you feel superior to any sin and cringe when hearing about another person's issues, you have crossed a dangerous line. Jesus forgave prostitutes and Pharisees. At the foot of the cross of Christ, both the perverted and the self-righteous need the same blood of Jesus to atone for their sin.[3]

There's a reason for such an attack on both sides in this area. It's because same-sex attraction attacks the very core assignment of identity and prohibits the person experiencing its attack from distinguishing what is true from what is a lie.

If the enemy can get us either struggling to know who we are or willing to heap judgment upon those who are struggling, he'll keep us all in the same place of stagnancy, with one party believing they're on some moral high ground.

The Christian who deals with same-sex attraction faces hard questions: *What if I never find sexually fulfilling love? What if I'm alone the rest of my life because I chose to be "obedient" to something I don't understand? What if I do end up living the way my body tells me it wants to and through that decision lose relationship with my family, friends, and God?*

What if I die alone and live my whole life as a quiet embarrassment to those who love me? What if God delivers me from this, and I can't find a person who is willing to take on my baggage?

I'm telling you, the darkness that accompanies this sin feels like being chained to a hamster wheel that keeps you running, exhausted, and going nowhere.

I realize that every now and then we tend to compare and contrast the darkness each sin brings. I'm not attempting to do that. I'm simply sharing what I know to be true about this area, and, since I've yet to find many people willing to have an honest conversation about it, I may as well bring it up. Because Lord knows I'm tired of Christians running from this dialogue. We may as well use my scars, so we can all start to heal.

As I journeyed through high school, I began to dive deeper and deeper into the darkness of my sexuality, which of course never ends there. That's when I became heavily addicted to pornography. I was depressed and meddling with suicidal thoughts, surrounding myself with people who only told me what I wanted to hear. I was an altogether angry person. I was angry with myself, with anyone who tried to correct me, with my parents for not knowing how to talk to me, and with any and every authority figure who had a hint of condescension or seemed as though they wanted a fight.

Okay, quick break from the serious stuff because this part is a little funny. We had some real charmers at my school, and, after I had been pushed and held up against a locker by a football player, I went to the assistant principal and principal to have them address the situation. They told me there was really nothing they could do about it, due to his position on the team and the necessity to have him start in a play-off game. As quickly as they told me that their hands were tied, I said, "Okay. Then where I'm concerned, your hands are going to be tied until I graduate. Because we all know I could go to the State Board about this and have both your jobs. So, if you see me having an off-campus lunch, you're going to let me have an off-campus lunch. If you see me in the hallways instead of in class, you will let me be. Because remember, your hands are tied, right?" I left the room. After that moment, I did pretty much whatever I wanted to do during my last two years of high school. I was the designated "off campus food picker-upper" for my friends and the few teachers I liked. I'm not going to say it was right, but I am saying it felt pretty good. Sue me.

Now back to the other 95% of my high school torment. To drown out the depression that was becoming louder, I became highly focused on succeeding in theatre. I spent every waking moment in the theatre department, being a part of all the drama (pun intended), dreaming about my future outside of Texas and away from all these "church people." During this time, I was mentored by people I shouldn't have been mentored by and spending time with friends who were just as broken as me. I was a whirling mess of emotion, frustration, and teenage angst, but mostly hurt. I was wounded by every comment made to me. I was hurt by my family because I didn't feel seen. I would find any reason to stay in the theatre department after school. I was quick to snap at any question my parents asked. When I would be invited to join my dad and brothers on "guy trips," I would dread them. I was combative with nearly every adult in my life and would shut my parents down any time they tried to give me advice. I was kicking my feet in all the privileged, annoying, little-white-privileged-kid ways. Let's call it what it was.

Then add to that behavior the normal struggles that go with being an adolescent. I was one big old ball of hurt. I was hurt when the only guy I developed feelings for going into my senior year rejected me, for which I attributed my being overweight and unattractive. This rejection then led me to lose nearly 70 pounds over the course of four months by simply not eating and running for as long as I possibly could multiple times a day. I was hurt because there weren't any of the grown and healthy men I'd seen around my brothers' lives wanting to be around my life. As I perceived it, no man wanted to take a chance to know or understand me.

But I was mostly hurt and upset with God. Although I hadn't surrendered my life and my thinking to Him yet, I had always known He was real. Jesus met me as a child several times in my room when I was too terrified to sleep. I had incredibly bad nightmares and would fall asleep looking at the door to my room, afraid that a robber was going to come in and kill me. I remember learning early on, in Sunday school classes and through my parents, if I just said Jesus' name, my fear would leave. I would lose a great deal of sleep due to my fear and the nightmares that followed, and I remember having the thought as a kid, *If I can't sleep and Jesus is who He says He is, I should be able to ask Him to put me to sleep.* I did, and Jesus, without fail, would slowly calm my mind in a matter of minutes. Without my realizing it, my brain would quickly calm down enough for me to rest, and I would be surrounded with a peace that was supernatural. Multiple times in my childhood I would have this sense, and not understand why, that I had my best friend sitting on the bed with me.

But, as I grew, and those memories became distanced by the amount of torment I was living with, I began to turn my hurt and anger toward God. I believed that He made me with the sexual desires I had and that He was punishing me for them. I thought, *It's as though God created me to then watch my misery.* I had prayed so many times asking Him to fix me, and I only seemed to grow unhealthier. By the time I started my senior year, I was, literally, hell bent. I wanted God to hurt for what I believed He had done to me, and I was going to live my life throwing it in His face along with any person in church or in my life who got in my way. It was a demonic and deeply low place in my life, fraught with romanticizing my own death and wanting to end my suffering.

Of course, I had no language to articulate my despair to my parents and no healthy influences to tell me actual truth. That is, until late fall of my senior year. Fall of 2007 will always be the time God came running after me in the most tangible and irrefutable way through my now amazing friend, Ryan.

Stick with me because I want to show you what it looks like to love someone in this lifestyle in a healthy, loving, truthful, and safe way. I met Ryan through another friend after my dad heard me sing in a few shows. My dad has always been an incredible champion of mine. He encouraged me to sing for someone at our church to get an honest opinion of my ability. When I did this, I was then directed to Ryan who was teaching voice lessons at the time and was thought to be someone who could help me. Let me tell you something ... God knew. Within five minutes of talking with Ry (my nickname for him), he looked me square in the eyes with no aversion or distrust and said, "You and I are going to be great friends." I was 17 at the time, and he was 27. I thought, *Yeah, right. Can't wait for him to not follow through and prove to me, yet again, I'm not welcome and don't belong in the Church.*

Much to my surprise, Ryan then proceeded to, in the words of Sister Mary Clarence via *Sister Act II*, "Dog me anyway." He called me about every day just to talk, check on me, and hear my thoughts. We'd meet regularly for dinner, and I would start to say something I wasn't sure how to communicate. Ryan would completely know what I meant and articulate my thoughts back to me with clarity. He understood me. (Sidebar: Ryan is possibly one of the top three funniest humans I know.)

After a few weeks with him just making me laugh and us getting to know each other, it became clear to me this guy was for real. One night over dinner, he could sense my hesitation in wanting to say, *But I feel like I'm gay, and I don't know how to not be and what to do with it.* As if Ryan was reading my mind or hearing the Holy Spirit as clear as could be, he said, "Hey, just so you know, I'm not going anywhere no matter what you do or who you think you are. We're doing life together, and that's it. You can't scare me away with anything." And he meant it. We left that dinner with me still not confiding in him. Yet, as Ryan pulled away from the restaurant, I immediately called him to say, "I think I'm gay, and I don't know what to do." He responded, "Hey Cav, guess what? It's okay, and we're going to figure it out together."

Over the next several months, Ryan began to mentor me in a way that made up for the years I had felt unseen. Before my friendship with Ry, I was a nerdy theatre kid with a few friends who mostly called me when they wanted to use my pool. With Ryan's friendship, I was staying out until the early morning hours in Dallas watching him play local shows and getting to know his crew of friends. Several of these people are now some of my nearest and dearest. These weren't nights spent partying. We spent time over breakfast at 1 or 2 in the morning that we lovingly called, "second dinners." I was in such a bad place at that time that Ryan was the one who cultivated the friend group that was allowed to spend time with me, just to provide me with complete safety. We talked about Jesus. I was able to ask questions without fear of rejection. For the first time, I found that people enjoyed my company solely because it was me. I realized I didn't have to be perfect to be loved.

After a few months of my back and forth, up and down, emotional roller coaster, I remember sitting across from Ry at the restaurant in Neiman Marcus (because have you had their popover rolls?). We were chatting over lunch about life, and he asked me a question I then answered a bit dishonestly. Next, he leaned over the table to ask me, "Aren't you tired?" I immediately broke down at the table because I knew exactly what he meant.

The truth:
I was tired.

I was extremely tired. I was tired of fighting. I was tired of running from God. I was tired of being miserable. I was sheer exhaustion made human.

A month later, my parents asked me to see an older couple who specialized in inner healing. My parents and others in my family benefited greatly from this ministry. I know, if you're unfamiliar with the process, it sounds super off base, but, I assure you, it's not. Inner healing is basically to address and help heal the hurtful things, voices, lies, and curses from a person's past. This couple was so kind, gentle, and not bothered by all the big bad things I had done or believed.

They asked me if I had ever accepted Christ. I thought back to so many times I'd said the prayer of salvation, but I knew I had never meant it. I had never fully given God my life. The couple simply said, "Well, let's just go ahead and take care of that now. Would you like to?" Even as I write about this experience, tears are welling up because I so wanted to surrender, and I was ready for Jesus to invade my world. I'll tell you something, like a flood, Jesus came into my life.

Within a few weeks, I had made enemies out of pretty much all my unhealthy relationships because they considered me "different" now that I was "too interested in God." It was incredible. In about a month, the Lord dismantled every unhealthy and toxic relationship I had. I was suddenly left with the group of friends I always wanted anyway.

The 180 that happened in me was honestly a bit startling to a lot of people. I had decided in the beginning of my senior year to "come out of the closet" to a few friends and teachers at school. After legitimately praying in counseling, asking the Lord to rid me of the thoughts and sexual desires I had, He did. In fact, I felt about a million pounds lighter. I was genuinely not attracted to guys anymore and had to start the fun task of telling the same people who I had come out to that I was now saved and set free. The looks, stares, laughs, and scoffs I got made for quite the symphony of senses. But I was okay and honestly not bothered because I knew the truth about myself now. I immediately jumped into serving at my church, traded my musical theatre scholarship in to go to Bible college, and started a new life.

I can't say that I've never struggled again because that would be an outright lie. Almost six months after the Lord changed my life, I fell prey to the same dark thoughts. It was a moment that was triggered by a weak period where I was flailing around, trying to understand what I was supposed to do with my life. I slipped back under the old mindset like getting under a comfortable blanket and allowed it to lull me back to darkness. The difference was, this time I didn't stay in the dark.

As I'm sure any believer will attest, once we choose Jesus, it doesn't mean that we still don't fall, slip up, or revert to unhealthy behaviors and thought processes. It means that now we are not held by them and that we are guaranteed to come back up for air again.[4] I did, and I do. But any time I doubt myself or start to even remotely believe God can't handle the brokenness I'm feeling, I remind myself of the truth that Elevation Worship communicates so well in their song, *Do It Again*:

I've seen You move, You move the mountains

And I believe, I'll see You do it again

You made a way, where there was no way

And I believe, I'll see You do it again.[5]

Lord, I thank You for the care with which You love each of us.

I thank You that You are so ready and willing to meet us wherever we are. You don't meet us in judgment or in condemnation, but in truth and love.

I know this chapter was a lot for my readers, Lord. I know there are probably questions, doubts, and arguments surrounding a good chunk of what I just presented.

So, I ask that You silence the voices and the accusations keeping readers from hearing what You truly want to communicate to them.

RELATIONSHIPS
AND OTHER IDOLS

3

If the inevitable intent of this book is that we would all either choose to walk in greater intimacy in relationship with the Lord or to even start a relationship with the Lord from the ground up, I believe it necessary to paint a truer picture of what's being offered in the person of Jesus. This is an unashamed baiting of a hook, and it's important to not insult your intelligence or waste your time by communicating anything else.

As I've hinted, our Millennial generation has been talked down to a great majority of our lives. We've been told to trust blindly, and that faith looks like *believing* before we see and *trusting* before we've reason to do so. Although I agree with the bare bones of that thinking and that believing will eventually lead to seeing, the way it's been communicated by the Church has not been awesome. In other words, we've been didactically told what to do and believe, but we've not seen those actions and beliefs authenticated in the people instructing us. This kind of communication leaves us feeling demeaned and less apt to trust authority figures. With this communication problem noted, we'll begin taking a practical look at earthly relationships and how they can form the foundations of our belief systems regarding what we can't see with our eyes, a lot of the time without our even realizing it.

I'm a firm believer in knowing context and being able to see how it affects a person's viewpoint. For instance, as I've previously mentioned, I didn't have the best time with athletes in high school. A very small percentage of them were horrible to me. Nevertheless, due to the formative nature of those few negative experiences, I have had a hard time with not immediately judging and placing labels on athletes as bigoted, hateful, stupid, and self-centered. Those are some awfully sweeping generalizations, right? Of course, they are. It wasn't until my early twenties that the Lord pried those dark accusations out of my head and separated the generalizations I was making from the isolated issues I had with a few young men. I realize you may be thinking, *So what exactly does this have to do with relationships?* Don't worry. I'm getting there.

Sometimes the aftermath of a negative experience impacts a person more than the actual experience. Now please hear me. I know people deal with real physical abuse, sexual assault, and worse. I am in no way trying to minimize those horrendous and egregious acts. I am simply saying that when we are hurt or are made to feel uncovered or unprotected by someone, whether that person is a friend, family member, or spouse, it's hard not to take that individual's action and ascribe it to a group.

For instance, it took me a long while to trust that I was genuinely wanted as a friend with no strings attached. This reticence was mainly because of a few significant relationships in high school. It has taken a great deal of unwiring in my head to stop thinking that the second I don't have something to provide, whether it be a service, skill, or even a jovial disposition, I've lost value to those nearest to me.

I think a lot of what kept me from knowing the Lord was not only a good chunk of hurt that I allowed to crystalize and turn into spiritual cataracts that kept me from seeing clearly, but also the assumptions I had about what a relationship with the Lord would look like that were based off what my earthly relationships appeared to be. My experience was that relationships were conditional, based on what I could provide, or how comfortable I could make someone feel by my actions or lack of neediness. I was a great asset to a friend group until I wasn't in the mood to crack the jokes that got me initiated into the group in the first place. I learned that most people don't know what to do with vulnerability. I thought it would be best for me to hold onto my own brokenness, try to sort it out by myself, and cover it with smiles and an, "I'm fine." I learned that conflict was something to be avoided at all costs, and to maintain about a quarter inch of depth with those around me because that was all most relationships could withstand. I learned that people couldn't be counted on and that they would, time and time again, prove to be disappointing. In that discovery, I learned to retreat further and further into myself as to not bother those around me and scare off the few friendships I had.

Because of my overall unhealth, I could not believe a relationship with God would look any different from any other failed relationship I had experienced. I was unable to believe in unconditional love, in the selfless nature of the work of Christ, or in the fact that Christians are called to be relational purists, giving of themselves freely because they have been freely given the purest relationship in Jesus.[6]

It's my belief that our society has no clue how to do pure relationship and that, if we did, we would have a much easier time believing that our purity in how we do life with one another is merely a shadow of the purity in how God wants to do life with us. The way most of us arrive at the place of wanting to develop a relationship with someone is, nine times out of ten, sourced in a trait or ability that potential friend may possess to service a need in us. It could be something as simple as wanting to know a person who is physically attractive, or wanting a funny friend, or a friend who is willing to be called on in an instant, or someone who has a great job, or someone who has influence, or someone well-connected, or someone who is a great listener. This is an understandable starting point for relationships as it's in our nature to be drawn to those who have something to offer, but that cannot be where pursuit in relationship ends. Once we start valuing a person based off what they bring to the table, then we start to see relationships as transactions. I bring "x" to the table. They bring "y" to the table. And the relationship works as long as that balance is kept. But what happens when we start thinking the giftings, influence, or characteristics we initially fell in love with in that one person are the standards and qualifying measures determining how and who we love in general?

What happens is, we make idols we will eventually hate. The person you start enjoying because they are funny, eventually becomes that one person who always has to have a joke, the one who you can't take seriously, or the one who isn't serious about anything. That friend who's always a great listener may have a day where they need to be listened to; and, because they are known as a listener but are suddenly not in "listening" mode, they let you down. When you're an influencer and tend to feel love by surrounding yourself with people who are always encouraging you, it's going to be those very "yes" people who end up wearing you out. That's because the natural progression of taking up an idol goes from interest, to obsession, to realization, to disgust. We're first interested by a thing or person that's shiny or different, then we become infatuated, then we have a moment where we realize its flawed nature, then we become disgusted that we ever ascribed value to something or someone so unworthy of our allegiance. That's why there are so many people who have relationships that are incredibly intense for a time, but quickly fall away. We make idols out of our relationships.

When we become good at accessing those people who will best serve our needs in a particular season, we can easily slip into the "rent-a-friend" mindset where we keep people around for as long as they serve our purpose. But the second we're made to work, change, or grow based on the needs of our friend(s), we can feel inclined to think it's not worth the work. Then, because we have deemed someone not worth the effort, it is an almost certain guarantee that the person on the receiving side of our walking away, ghosting, or minimization is going to feel unworthy. What this experience teaches is that a person's value and ability to be loved is based solely off what they do.

I realize there are healthy times to walk away from relationships and the choice to do so is often a necessary part of life. However, if you're someone who tends to have cyclical relationships that last for a year or two at a time, I'd argue that you're one who tends to be drawn more to those people who service your relational needs. When someone has served their purpose, needs something from you, or asked for change, you don't know quite what to do. That's because we are incredibly "me" focused in our living and being.

See, this cycle continues and shows itself in a myriad of ways. For instance, you may be someone who doesn't let go of people when they upset you or do something disagreeable. In fact, you may be someone who has become more addicted to being the victim, so you're drawn to relationships that repeat what you believe to be true. Both the "rent-a-friend" person and the "victim-in-relationship" person are in equally unhealthy places.

One effect of how we tend to do relationship on a natural level is a tendency to misjudge God's character. We assume God operates with us the same way we operate with each other. This is not the case. The way He does everything, let alone relationship, is higher than us and our thoughts on how relationships should look.[7]

See, God doesn't need for you to be anything other than who you are and doesn't look for perfection before He gives you His approval.[8] God loves us without a manipulative agenda or sinister motive. In fact, even what many people would view as restrictions in the Christian faith are really loving boundaries which reflect God's desire for us to live healthy and full lives on earth. God's boundaries for us don't service some heavenly need He has for us to be a certain way before He will love us.[9] Jesus secured the way for us to have relationship with God the Father and for Him to have relationship with us. Jesus was perfection made human who willingly died to redeem us.[10] When He rose from the dead three days later, He also confirmed the fact that God has no ulterior motive other than to love and be in relationship with you and me. He doesn't love us dependent on how much time we spend in prayer, how long we've gone without sinning, or what we can do to service the Kingdom. His love for us does not depend on our goodness at all.

The shocking truth of the Gospel is that the person who accepts Jesus gets the same approval and love God the Father gives His Son.

When God looks at me, He sees His own perfection because I'm in Christ.[11]

God loves us wholly and unconditionally, and that love is what empowers us to change. It's what draws us into deeper relationship with Him and calls us to a higher place in life. It doesn't look like some abstract feeling of being okay, which is what I think mainstream culture has trivialized faith to be. This popular trivialization of faith makes sense because our natural inclination is to want to feel okay at the end of the day. We want to feel secure in our goodness and to believe that, should the world go up in flames, we have enough approval from some *Higher Power* in the sky who will look at us at the end of it all and call us "good" based on our own merits. In contrast, the Gospel says God approves of me based on Christ's merit given to me as a free gift of grace.[12] In other words, I don't save myself by trying to be good enough. Jesus saves me because He is good enough.

Yes, of course, my faith provides assurance, approval, and a quiet peace that makes me feel at rest when I've no reason to feel peace. But, through faith, I also have Someone who is actively speaking to me and through me to people. My faith means I've chosen an active relationship with Jesus.

When I'm walking in passive relationship with Christ, I know I'm still saved and on my way to heaven, but I'm probably not spending time praying. Because I'm not talking to God, I'm also probably not listening to His voice. I'm probably not spending time worshipping, doing things that are filling my soul's stomach. I slip into a kind of spiritual cruise control. An active relationship with Christ, in contrast, is filled with daily adventures where I'm more concerned about finding people TO love as opposed to finding people who will love me. It's a paradigm shift because, in my relationship with Christ, I'm receiving wholly and freely from Him what I know I can never receive, what no one can ever receive, from a person.[13] We were never meant to have our emotional and relational needs perfectly fulfilled through human relationships.

Of course, God uses people to show us elements of His love for us and, in doing so, shows us how to love others better. Still, we are meant to know love in its truest and purest form from God.[14] From that place, we begin to live differently and realize that life is more than doing life only with people who are easy to love. It then becomes a gift when someone enters our lives and needs special attention, time, or a listening ear. We stop seeing these opportunities as burdens. They are avenues to give to others the perfect love we've already received.

God came to earth to flip our perspective on its head and to rewire us altogether. Christ came to show us what pure relationship can do in healing a broken heart, in pulling someone up to a higher level, in showing genuine and unadulterated love. When a person lives in this kind of pure relationship, their life points upward and always calls back to the original source of that pure relationship: Christ.

We can't look at the fractured bits of how we do earthly relationships and use them to infer how we think God loves us or how He wants to engage with us. He wants an active relationship where we can both speak and be heard, where we feel safe to bring our worries and the darkest moments of our life to Him, where we can work with Him as a team to love a dying world around us, where we can find security and a strength not always given in human relationships.

A relationship with Christ is more than fire insurance and nothing less than the greatest relationship you'll ever experience. Although it pains me to admit it, and I share in responsibility for this reality: this truth has not been modeled as well as it could be. In large part, Christians have traded in their calling to love fiercely for the right to be right. With that choice, many Christians have made an idol out of behavioral preferences that Christ never called us to monitor or to enforce. We're meant to first love God with every part of us and to love our neighbor as we would love ourselves.[15] If the reader has experienced hardship at the hand of a Christian, on behalf of those of us who have not been the best light-bearers and witnesses of what God came to be in our lives, please forgive us.

The wonder of a gracious and merciful God who sits with the "dirty" and the "put together" alike while loving them the same is what we should be representing. That is the call for us in relationship and in life. Anything less is a watered down, tempered version of the Gospel that misrepresents the message of God, and, in doing so, misrepresents God altogether. I'm not about that life.

I'm not under the delusion that sinning is something I no longer do. Aware of my own struggles, I handle the nature of sin with delicate gloves. I write about sin, knowing I need grace. For just a little recap: Jesus said, if I even hate someone in my heart, I've murdered them all the same.[16] There seems to be a lot about the human heart God wants to redeem; in fact, He really wants to redeem it all. If He had wanted us to live our lives based solely on actions, He would have left a book of rules. Oh wait, He did; it's called the Old Testament. But more than a book of rules, it is a blueprint for us to see not only His power during our unwillingness to obey, but also our inability to keep a perfect record on our own.

I know that many people in our culture today, and especially young Christians, tend to find the Old Testament contradictory to the New Testament. If we look at them both on a macro level, identifying major themes, characters, and overall tone, it's easy to make a sweeping judgment about what God was intending to communicate in both testaments. We see that God "is angry" throughout the Old Testament, so we then say, *Well, then God's an angry God. Look at how He punished the Israelites. Look at all the insanely hard-to-follow rules He put in place. If He's God, then why didn't He know that His people would have such a difficult time being faithful and staying true to Him? If He really is a loving God, then how could He be so difficult to His own people?* These questions are just the tip of the iceberg when trying to make sense of the God of the Old Testament.

Then Jesus enters the story at the top of the New Testament. We see Hope Himself burst on the scene. With every word Jesus utters, lives change around Him. We see that our victory as believers is tangible and possible through the life, death, and resurrection of Christ.[17] We see applicable principles and much more easy-to-follow lines of thinking. Before we know it, we might slowly start to believe that the New Testament eradicates the need for the Old. We start to believe that the God of the Old Testament and New Testament are not the same.

I understand this line of thinking as I've personally contended with it a great deal. I'll find myself in the middle of Leviticus or Numbers or reading some line of genealogy and literally stop to pray, "Okay, Lord. This isn't my favorite thing to read. So, I'm asking that You make it alive to me and show me what You want to show me." When I flip my perspective from trying to make sense of it to getting out of it what the Lord wants to show me, it frees me up to see all sorts of great truths. Then, reading the Bible becomes this beautiful game of hide and seek.

Sometimes, if we're not careful, we can choose to believe God is intentionally hiding from us, as if He has some cruelty in Him that would withhold from us the goodness of Himself. This is simply not His character. When God removes Himself from plain sight, it forces us to look for Him differently. Not only that, but it gives us the joy of finding Him because we've searched for Him.

I'm working on this chapter a few days after Easter, and, when I think about the way the Lord wants us to search for Him, I can't help but think about Easter egg hunts. My family currently has nine sweet grandchildren; their ages range from seven years old to younger. Easter at our house is a big event. My mother goes all out on this day. She spends an inordinate amount of time preparing, making sure she has little gifts and things especially for each grandchild. She thinks intentionally about what each one of them would love to open or receive, and she lavishes it on them. When it comes to hiding the Easter eggs, a few of us adults will sneak out into the backyard and start "hiding" eggs. I put quotes around this word because it's really not hiding the eggs. We put eggs in a general area toward which we then guide each child. We make sure that the treasures are not immediately seen, but not impossible to find. The younger children tend to pretty much have their eggs out in the open grass, while the older ones have to look through more plants and pay a little more attention to find their surprises. The whole time the children are searching, Sweet Mama and Poppy (the names the grandchildren call my parents) are smiling and loving their exploration and the joy on their faces when they find a treasure. When a child starts getting colder on the hunt or walks right past a treat, my mother or father will gently guide them back to the area where the eggs can be found.

I know I've spent a bit of time with this illustration, but it's because it's so important for us to know the Father's heart for us when it comes to His Word. God has treasures and eggs of wisdom for us hidden throughout His Word. He's so good, that there is new revelation and insight in every chapter and in every phrase ... if we're looking for it.[18] As we grow and mature in the Lord, we learn that the search is part of the fun. We don't become overwhelmed when we're not beholding a glistening, bright, and shiny egg full of goodies right away because we know that God is going to guide us to treasures. God sets His love upon us and is passionate about showing us His goodness even when it doesn't look that way on the surface. I mean, can we talk about the Israelites? They could never seem to get it right. Time after time, they disobeyed, were punished, and redeemed to only then repeat the cycle. God never gave up on them or decided to stop being their God.

So, when we talk about the sin nature and our struggle with it, we really have to step away from the idea that God's expectation of us is perfection. We must take the Word in its entirety, knowing it's a complete story with a beginning, middle, and end. We have to stop believing that we'll never be good enough because God certainly wouldn't approve of our x, y, or z sin. We have been redeemed through Christ and now don't have to make atonement for our own sins as the Israelites did. Jesus made atonement for us once and for all on the cross.[19] That grace doesn't mean that we live like hellions and aren't obedient to the conviction of the Holy Spirit and the Word, but it does mean we're off the tightrope. We get to walk freely and boldly with the assurance that, when we sin, we are forgiven.

So, when we read the Old Testament from a place of gratitude and out of a longing to understand more of this amazing God who redeemed us back to Himself, we're able to be gobsmacked by details that seem contrary to what we expect. We can ask God to reveal what He chooses to reveal. Because He's a good Father, He may hide Himself from us, but not forever. He loves, loves, LOVES being found by us.

There isn't a single cruel thing about the Lord.

He is justice, righteousness, love, redemption, mercy, grace, covering, freedom, wholeness, and stability at all times, in all things. And that is just the very beginning of all He is.

If we're looking for God's goodness in the Old Testament, we start to see foreshadowing of Jesus, visions that are then fulfilled in the New Testament.[20] We see that God's discipline is only ever meant to serve God's redemptive purpose. We see that, at every turn, God uses us in our weakness for His glory. We see that God chooses a lowly and humble shepherd boy like David to not only defeat a giant enemy, but to make a king. Our Savior comes from David's lineage.

When God requires a seemingly impossible sacrifice from us, it is only ever meant to show us His goodness in a new way. Remember when Abraham was asked to sacrifice his son, Isaac?[21] Talk about craziness, right? Not only does Abraham agree, but so does his son. I mean, can you imagine anything more horrible to be asked than that? I can't even fathom it. I'm a bit of a crier, and, even as I'm writing, this revelation is hitting me again in a new way. It's heartbreakingly beautiful. Their hearts were so committed to obeying the Lord just because He asked.

As they are atop a mountain, right before Abraham is about to plunge the knife into his son, God stops him and provides a ram stuck in a thicket to be sacrificed in Isaac's stead. God never intended on Abraham actually sacrificing his son. God wanted to see Abraham and Isaac's faith at work. Because Abraham was willing, as was Isaac, we have this beautiful parallel of what it was like for God, the Father, and Jesus, the Son, to be atop a hill called Golgotha. This time, however, the sacrifice wasn't stopped. This time God didn't provide a ram in the thicket to take Jesus' place. A ram wouldn't have finished the job of redemption, but the spotless Lamb called Jesus, on the other hand, did. Now when you think about the story like that, it's a little less about God's cruelty to ask Abraham to do something so apparently insane, and more about God wanting us to understand His heart and the way it broke when He did to His Son what He would never require us to do.

I am still figuring out a lot and trying to make sense of what doesn't seem plausible. In doing so, God has met me in some incredible ways. But it isn't because I have lived perfectly or free from temptation. On the contrary, I have fought with depraved, demonic, and downright ungodly thoughts, feelings, and actions I've had to mull my way through to meet Jesus. That's where the victory and treasure is, that place we get to where we don't allow our stumbling to keep us stuck. When I think about the amount of time I've wasted living in the muck of how yesterday's sin impacted my outlook and willingness to grow, I am saddened.

Many of my struggles with the Lord are struggles to believe correctly about myself. While this struggle is real, I would argue that an even larger portion of my stagnant periods in life have come from my unwillingness to let myself off the hook long enough to see that the sky isn't crumbling and that nothing and no one is keeping me from moving forward. Often, we think that our big moments, revelations, and encounters with the Lord come from our striving to experience them. We almost want to feel as though we've earned the great victory we're hoping to see one day. If I don't guard my heart, I may think God is proud of my self-loathing and frustration because then He knows how really sorry I am about my sin, like my penance earns His forgiveness. This thinking is incorrect.

A person can drown in a few feet of water if they don't realize they can simply stand up. Our spiritual lives are no different. Sometimes we can become so consumed with contending with one sin or recent failure that we drown in hopelessness. Stand up. It doesn't mean that you don't have to wade through junk and difficulties to keep moving. But, standing up does mean that junk and those difficulties do not kill you. They are now simply things you are working through as opposed to things that are stopping or suffocating you. If we can change our perspective and see ourselves in context, we'll have a much easier time not being overwhelmed by our own brokenness.

As children of God, we exist in the context of a good and loving Father who is patient and not bothered by our frailty. We exist in the context of a God who said He would turn ALL things for the good of those who love Him and are called according to His purpose.[22] So breathe. Pick your head up and keep moving forward. I believe we've all spent enough time drowning in the kiddie pool.

To pick your head up and move forward, it's important to know what it looks like to walk through something as opposed to being stuck in it. Lucky for you, I've spent a lot of my life stuck, so I have a little bit of insight here. One of the first helpful shifts to make in your mind is to realize that whatever seems so big and looming at any given moment is always going to seem that way until you change your sightline. The devil will always bring the small issues, big issues, and all the other issues in front of your face so they're the only things you see. Who needs a magnifying glass when the devil is quick to do the job for us?

The problem is, we think we have no say in what we see, where our attention is focused, or on what we fixate. It feels almost as if someone is holding a newspaper directly in front of our eyes where all we can read is the headline, "FAILURE." We see the headline and are not able to see the surrounding context or how small that one headline is in comparison to the other headlines in the paper. What if we were able to pull the newspaper a little further away, read it in its entirety, and had the right to turn the page when we wanted? We can.

The enemy's intention is to keep you as far away from the Lord, heaven, and your purpose as he possibly can. To accomplish this intention, he will take small issues and magnify them in your face until you believe failing is what you do and stop trying. The devil wants to paralyze you by the headline, playing it as a loop over and over in your head. He'll keep printing the headline unless he knows that's not an area he can win anymore. He'll then turn the page and try to focus your attention on another seemingly tragic headline in your life, and he will do this for the entirety of your life, if you let him. He'll also do a fun li'l bit every now and then where he'll turn back to a page you thought you read before and point out a headline from your past. You'll think, *Now, wait a sec. I've already dealt with this struggle. Why is this issue trying to overtake me again?* When those moments happen, the way we respond is crucial. If we give an old headline attention, we're more than likely going to start re-reading it like we did in the past. I'm not meaning to discourage you, far from it. I just don't have time to hear or speak anything other than the truth, so I hope you'll hear my directness in the love with which it is intended.

We have been given authority over the devil, so it's important we exercise it well. If I have authority over the enemy, that means I may not have authority over the headlines shoved in my face, but I do have the right to tell the devil to take his hands out of my face and turn the page when I say. He may try to steal my focus, call my attention to only the death in my life, and try to make me believe it's all I am. But I know his headlines are only a small part of a much larger story. I can look at them and say, "Well actually, that may be the tidbit you pulled out of my life to focus on, but it's a red herring in my story because God says differently about me. In fact, God says ...

I'm His child, Jesus' friend, that I'm not condemned.[23]

I'm not dirty. I've been washed clean by the blood of the Lamb.[24]

I'm redeemed, justified, and accepted.[25]

I'm a saint, a fellow heir with Christ, and that, because of Him, I am being sanctified.[26]

I'm on my way to victory through Jesus.[27]

I'm a new creation.[28]

I'm not a slave.[29]

I'm set free and gifted with every spiritual blessing in the heavenly places.[30]

I'm chosen and blameless before Him, forgiven by Jesus' grace.[31]

I'm seated with Him in heavenly places.[32]

I'm His workmanship, and I was created to do good things.[33]

I'm a member of the Body of Christ, which means I share in His promises.[34]

I'm confident and bold, a citizen of heaven.[35]

I'm complete in Jesus. The literal peace of God guards my heart and mind.[36]

So, have a seat, Devil. You've got the wrong headline.

This is my identity in Christ, but the enemy tempts me to forget who I am. The Word of God is my weapon in this battle to remember and live in the Truth. There's a reason the Bible describes reading the Word as an actual washing of one's mind.[37] Think about it. If you only showered once a month, and someone called you "nasty," you would probably respond, "You know, I can see your point." You'd begin to smell like the food you ate, what you were around, and your perspiration. Your body would become a magnet for filth. Also, an interesting point is that there are a few studies showing how a person, after about a month of not bathing, develops a natural protective film on the skin and starts producing natural oils which moisturize the body. Oh yeah, and, apparently, you don't smell anymore either. Now there are probably a few hippies-at-heart who would sign up for that, but showering regularly and maintaining a level of cleanliness is not only important for you ... but also for the people who have to smell you. Clearly, I like to beat a metaphor into the ground, and, to be honest, you're welcome.

The point is that washing in the Word is the healthiest thing we can do for ourselves. It rids us of the scents and aromas of sin that try to linger on us. It also changes our perspective. It is an actual mental and spiritual shower. The more you shower in the Word, the cleaner you will feel, smell, and live. If you don't believe me, or even if you do, I'd suggest you try something. Challenge yourself to start reading just three chapters of the Bible a day. Then, depending on the day you've had, you may want to dig in even deeper.

I know at certain points in my life, when it seems I'm contending with something especially evil or nasty, I automatically up my Bible intake. I remember talking to one of my best friends in a really dark moment of my life, and I was like, "I'm not going to lie. It's not even an option for me to not be in the Word today. In fact, I currently need to be in the Word 3–4 times a day because I'm contending that hard to keep my mind and perspective correct."

When I'm in the Word, I'm unstoppable. Then there are times when a day or two will go by, and I'll be thinking, *Wow! I didn't even get in the*

Word today, and I haven't had one harmful thought or done one thing with which God wouldn't be okay. Then, as if my legs are swiftly being kicked out from under me, I'll fall prey to something. It happens so fast, and the reason is that my defenses are down. I start smelling like sin again because I haven't been washing in the Word. Just like that, the enemy sees an open door and takes it. So, we read and trust the headlines in the Word and keep the Truth as our perspective, a sure strategy against the lies of the enemy.[38]

Lord, I am so grateful that You give us the joy of relationship. I ask, Lord, that we would see relationship and its value in correct priority. I know You desire one-on-one, individual, beautifully intimate friendship with us. I also know that, when I receive my value from You, I don't look for it elsewhere. I ask that You reveal Your pure heart and the freedom that comes when we wholly find our value in You and You alone.

4

I didn't surrender my life to the Lord until I was 18, and yes, I do mean, surrender. Before we talk about surrender and what it looks like, can I let you in on a secret? The whole point of God wanting us to surrender to Him is that it puts us back in proper design and alignment with the actual order of things. When we stay in our lane, so to speak, we get out of the way. When we get out of the way, we begin to clearly see Him and ourselves. We are not god. God is God.

Aside — if you're someone who is reading this and fundamentally disagrees with the Christian worldview, that's okay. If nothing else, this content might help open you up to more understanding. Because I love you, I'll explicitly state my intention behind writing this book: I want you to experience and surrender to Jesus. That is exactly my intention.

We have an inherent tendency as humans to feel entitled. We feel entitled to explanation, to kindness, to opportunity, to vacation time, to romantic relationships, to "fair" wages, to eating what we want, to living however we choose. This natural bent toward entitlement serves as a disconnect with God.

The sooner we realize God doesn't owe us anything, the sooner we start to see Him for who He truly is. He doesn't owe us an explanation for the battles we face. He doesn't owe us freedom. He doesn't owe us kindness. He doesn't owe us eternity with Him. He doesn't owe us healing. He doesn't owe us relationship. He doesn't owe us contentment. He doesn't owe us salvation ... but these are all things He freely gives.

Surrender is the key which unlocks the *Alice in Wonderland* rabbit hole of grace that drops you into a reality like you've never known. Surrender's purpose is to lead us into fullness. What we view as surrender, God sees as an exchange — our will for His. If you're struggling to let go of something or someone in your life to surrender to Christ, let me level with you: that thing, position, substance, experience, pleasure, or relationship is dead outside of divine purpose and calling. I understand some people might think that claim is ridiculous and trite, naïve and "something for simpler people," or, one of my personal favorites, "what some people need to believe to cope." Here's honesty: If I gained the whole world, but I didn't have Jesus, I'd have nothing.[39] People who know they are a "hot mess" don't bother me. I worry most for people who don't see their own insufficiencies and need for the One who is bigger than themselves.

When I think about how deadened we have become to our own needs and actual issues, I think of leprosy. Nowadays leprosy is quite curable and isn't seen as a life-threatening illness. But before the wonders of modern medicine and discoveries of treatment became widely accessible, this disease was a violent killer. The disease itself is a slow bacterial infection that sometimes takes years before its symptoms manifest. It attacks the nerves and ends up deadening the victim's ability to feel pain altogether. In the past, it was common that those with leprosy would lose limbs, stab or cut themselves, and lose fingers and other extremities without feeling a thing. We currently live in the middle of people with deadened spiritual nerves that have been numbed and sedated by an inability to deal with, look at, address, or heal wounds. Infection grows in our hearts and heads, and we are blithely unaware.

Even as you're reading this paragraph, I imagine a rolodex of memories is flipping through your mind. You could be remembering your childhood where prayer and believing God at His word was normal and beautiful. You could remember conversations from years ago where you knew you were close to a breakthrough, but now you've forgotten what that feels like. You could be remembering what it was like when you walked down the church aisle and told God you wanted Him to have your whole heart. These memories and things we know deep down to be true are constantly trying to bubble up to the service. Let those memories come in the name of Jesus.

We have been taught to view our younger years as the "figuring it out" time. Many of us, while searching for our purpose, look at the simplicity of faith and its place in our lives as being small-minded or juvenile. If you think that sincere faith is a sign of immaturity, or that a person of faith is uneducated or weak, that's unfortunate. We live in a time when education is the foremost creditor of ideals, and yet some of the most miserable people I've ever met are the most educated. I've never known knowledge itself to empower a person to love more. To be perfectly honest, I don't look for master's degrees when I need advice from someone. I look for advice from a person who knows how to love people. A degree has never asked how I'm doing. I've never met a history teacher whose knowledge of the Cold War empowered them to love outside of themselves. Knowledge may be power, but it has no power of its own. You can give reason after reason for not believing in God. You can use knowledge to explain away or backup pretty much whatever you want. So yes, knowledge is power in the hands of those using it, but knowledge without God holds zero power.[40]

Knowledge doesn't hold the power to heal a broken heart.

Knowledge doesn't restore marriages.

Knowledge doesn't reclaim a childlike joy in someone who hasn't smiled in years.

Knowledge doesn't have the authority to cast out darkness in someone.

Knowledge doesn't know how to comfort a grieving mother after a miscarriage.

Knowledge doesn't know how to hold an abandoned child in their weakest state and whisper peace and security.

Knowledge doesn't bring quiet peace to the person who has lost everything.

Knowledge doesn't care for the orphans, the widows, the poor, and those who are destitute and longing for a home.

Knowledge, in and of itself, is powerless.

I realize we often associate power with influence, celebrity, wealth, public position, political prowess, and overall ability. That is not the power I'm interested in discussing. In fact, that's not real power at all. I'm talking about the power that impacts, engages, softens, heals, and loves on the hearts of the hurting and whole alike. That's the power which interests me. We have enough people in the world using their "power" to advance themselves and their agendas, but who don't know how to look someone in the eye and genuinely empathize to save their life. I'm here to advance Christ's agenda. Let that be clear.

Even as I'm writing this, I literally just got a call from a friend who has recently started pursuing a relationship with the Lord with her whole heart. We've been friends for a few years and have had a lot of hard and difficult conversations that the Lord was gracious enough to bless. It is amazing to see the ACTUAL power of Jesus at work in her life. She didn't even know that I was in the middle of this chapter, and, through tears, she told me how God supernaturally intervened in a seemingly impossible situation. She said, "I just can't believe this. He's really so good, and I'm over here thinking, 'But I don't know why. I don't deserve it.'" We laughed together, and, as tears welled up in my eyes, I was reminded of my deepest desire which is that everyone would come to know Jesus, HIS power, and to be staggered by how specifically and especially He loves us.

My friend spent years in and around the Church community, but it wasn't until she completely surrendered her way of thinking that she saw freedom in her own life. She wondered for years, *What does a Christian look like? How is God going to use me? Do these people who say they love Jesus really love Him? Do Christians just tolerate me or love me, too?* At the exact moment she gave up trying to figure everything out, God arrested her heart. She is now seeing the power of God at work in her life, and the joy and deepening love Christ is bringing is beautiful to watch. Now, the sheer contentment on her face and even the lightness in the way she walks is night and day different from what it was. Because Jesus.

The initial surrender of "my way of thinking and being" to Christ's way is sometimes portrayed as this sweet and quiet prayer that comes off our tongue like a piece of Shakespearean prose ... and I'm sure that's sometimes how it happens. I haven't personally experienced that, but sure, why not?

As of late I've known surrender to look a bit different. I know my own initial surrender looked like a spiritual battle that came in the form of every bit of breaking I could stand. It came in the late hours of the night when I had exhausted all options and places to turn to outside of God. It came in the form of tears which flowed from the deepest part of me until I tired myself out.

I've learned that God will let us run ourselves into a mental wall until we break. Once we've broken, the Healer is instantly on site to build a masterpiece where our old self used to be. Our brokenness partners with the smallest amount of faith that says, "God, I can't do life like this anymore. I'm exhausted, and I've nowhere else to go." That's when the shift happens in us. It seems small at first and trivial to simply change your mind about something. Incidentally, the Greek word for *repent* in the New Testament is *metanoeo'* which means "to change one's mind." So, when you lay down the fact that you think you have it figured out, that's when the magic of the Kingdom of God begins to work in you. So maybe laying down our right to understand and to know everything is more paramount than we think.

See? *Repentance* isn't such a big, bad, and scary religious word ... already another Christianese word explained. Repentance is admitting to yourself and to the Lord that you're wrong, incorrect, or don't know a right way of being in a given situation. You surrender to the fact that you are not God and have no business trying to play as though you are.

I had to become so discontent with myself and my own head and heart that I wanted to receive someone else's. This is a point to which most people come. Now, whether this point leads a person farther from or further to the feet of Jesus is dependent on the individual. I first had to decide that my will no longer mattered in comparison to His will. Once I surrendered, I then chose to believe God was good.

This is where I've found most people get hung up. There isn't a single person I've met who hasn't struggled with trusting the goodness of God. We see terror happening all over the world, hear the unkindness in people who claim to be followers of Jesus, mourn the deaths of people we love most, collect dashed hopes and dreams like badges, and we hold, like heavy chains, the gathering anger and desire to blame someone for the brokenness in and around us. The hard questions might be some of the following:

"If God is good, why did we just have another pointless bombing?"

"If God is good, why did my mother die when I was an infant?"

"If God is good, why would He allow such evil people to live in the world?"

"If God is good, why have I fought depression my whole life?"

The goodness of God cannot be defined by evil or lack of perceived goodness in the world. Evil has no part of Him.

To see the goodness of God, we have to choose to see it.

We say and hear, "You find what you're looking for." If you stopped and genuinely asked God to show you His goodness, you would start to see it shine through the darkness that seems so real and tangible. That's a promise.[41]

But if you're just looking for an *Operation Dumbo Drop* of money, relationships, or fulfilled dreams, then chances are, you'll miss Him. If that's what you're looking for, you're looking for the wrong thing. His goodness looks much more like a settling of the heart and a peace that surpasses understanding than it does a parachute of blessing. Once you choose to believe God is good, you'll start to experience joy when you shouldn't, peace when it doesn't make sense, provision when you don't deserve it, and blessings in areas you never dreamed possible.

The goodness of God isn't that you find the perfect spouse. The goodness of God is that even when you don't get what you want or think you need, or even when you do experience great loss, Jesus is still with you. The Source of all goodness, beauty, and truth is with you. No matter what happens, Jesus is yours, and you are His. You know what that means? No matter what you may lose, you can't ultimately lose the Source of ultimate value, purpose, and identity in your life. The most dangerous person to the enemy is the person who knows that, because of Jesus, they have nothing to lose and everything to gain.[42] We've got to stop thinking that the goodness of God is monetized by how easy or great our life is on the surface. The goodness of God is the quiet assurance of the fact that I am being upheld in any and every season of my life and into eternity. THAT is His goodness.[43]

I may as well let you know now: having relationship with God is the wildest, most rewarding adventure you will ever have. Choosing to believe in and see His goodness is one of the hardest daily decisions we must make. He will hide at times and make you search for and choose to believe in His goodness when it doesn't make sense. He knows that this search deepens our roots and strengthens our spiritual bones. God pursues our hearts, romances our minds, provides escape routes out of darkness, and gently calls our names. The point of Jesus coming to earth was to break every kind of bondage separating us from Him.[44] God's a Chain-breaker, and don't you forget it.

The decision to first believe that God is good is one that's made in hope and, a lot of times, without the tangible proof one might think necessary for that decision. But, if all the earth is God's handiwork,[45] then your decision to follow Christ is only in response to the evidence that's already surrounding you. Faith is responding to an invisible, but evident, God. To put your faith in God means a heart shift, perspective change, and a new resolution to believe the character and sovereignty of God. This is the action of faith. And yes, we are required to put our faith in action. If you're afraid to surrender and even now feel your heart resisting it, don't worry. I'll tell you how you can surrender by a power you don't have to generate in your own strength, intellect, or feelings: simply ask the Holy Spirit to ignite faith in Christ in you. Especially if there's a part of you that feels hesitant to know the Gospel, ask the Holy Spirit to break through your walls. If you ask Him, He will. That's an actual promise. [46] It may not be immediate and instant like you want, but He will transform your heart. Sometimes slowly and sometimes like a tidal wave, God will make Himself known to any heart longing to know Him. If you want to watch your world change, start thanking God for His goodness in the middle of your darkest moments and during your questioning.

Something that seems increasingly difficult is to surrender to the sovereignty of God without a great deal of understanding, especially for us Millennials. That's how our finite, limited brains work. You may think, *I need to have all the facts. I need all the answers to my questions before I give my life over to Jesus.* No, you don't. That's just a more grown-up way of stalling to avoid surrender and real change.

This adventure, one I wouldn't trade for anything, all begins with that simple yet costly word, *surrender*. Surrender your ways of thinking that don't put God in the highest place and surrender your right to have every answer before giving Jesus your "yes."

Lord, thank You for surrender and the fruit it produces in our lives. Thank You for taking our weakness and exchanging it for Your strength. I'm grateful that truly yielding to You renews our awareness of Your tenderness toward us. I know surrender is almost a modern curse word and that the last thing most of us want to be seen as is in need. But, Lord, we do need You. So, I ask right now that You would reveal to the reader their need for You.

GRACE RECEIVED = GRACE TO GIVE

I f you're one who finds it difficult to understand the applicable nature of Jesus to your everyday life, start here. He's a big fan of relationship and an even bigger fan of you. That should be reason enough to try and get to know Him a little better. I'm not talking about some abstract or ethereal version of relationship wherein we coax ourselves into believing we're having conversations with God, but in actuality we're just making ourselves feel good. That is the lie that will be at the forefront of anyone's mind who is contending for a starting point in faith. I am talking about an actual relationship ... with conversations, growth, and real freedom.

I grew up in an incredibly strong, faith-based home. Now, if this is possibly one of your first attempts at understanding the larger picture of faith, let me make a clear distinction. The world would call Christianity at its core "religion," but that's incorrect. This is where, if you're someone who has grown up in church and had a hurtful experience, you could easily add a sneer and sarcastic tone while saying, "It's a relationship."

See, this is what a lot of Christians will say but not live; so, the confusion of how Christianity differs from other world religions exponentially grows. But I'll explain this distinction as briefly as I can. There is no other religion but Christianity, be it Buddhism, Islam, or Hinduism, where the god or "higher power" sacrifices its own life for the sake of its followers. There is no other religion where forgiveness is freely given with no strings attached. Most religions have the goal, "Do right, and you will be rewarded rightly. Do wrong, and you'll pay a price."

Christianity, in contrast, is not about a list of rules we follow to be blessed, loved, accepted, known, cared for, or redeemed. Christianity is the story of a good God who wants to redeem a broken world back to Himself. It's about a God who created humanity out of His own joy. It's not about an angry god who is ready to smite the nearest sinner, but about the goodness of God who rescues people and whose love empowers them to be completely new and whole. Christianity is the only world religion where a person is rescued by trusting what God has done for them, not what they've done for God. Christianity is not about trying to be "good enough" for God. It's about Jesus who dies in place of sinners, takes their punishment on Himself, and gives them His own goodness.[47]

Christians don't work *for* God's acceptance. They work *from* God's acceptance.

I've gotten into more conversations with people of differing viewpoints over the past few years, and the biggest hang-up I find is when people want to lump my God, the one of the Old and New Testament, in with the god of Islam, with the principles of Buddhism, or any other religion. It also really grinds my gears when I hear people say that their belief in a Higher Power is the same as a relationship with God. The issue with that thinking, beyond its ambiguity, is that it doesn't put a face or identity on what is believed. It's a cheap way of saying, "I believe in the fact that there is something or someone greater than me, but I don't want to submit to it/them/him/her." It's such a formless belief system.

Then others will keep to the idea of a god in one religion being the same across all religions. Some people say the God of the Bible and Allah of Islam are really the same, that they came from the same origins, and they're just different names for the same god. To that I will gently respond, these two faiths are no more similar than two guys named Jeff living on opposite sides of the world. You can't read both the Bible and the Quran and genuinely view Jesus and Allah as the same deity. Since we live in a world that takes the ideals and opinions of other people and regurgitates them with individual biases, I would like to encourage you to read, research, and know for yourself beyond just simply believing what I say.

I am in no way claiming to have all the answers, or even a great chunk of them. I am simply sharing what I have spent my life trying to understand and who God has been and is in my life. But I don't want you to assume I haven't given thought to many other ideals than the ones with which I was raised. In fact, because I was raised by strong Christians, I probably wanted to rebel against Christianity even more; add to that the fact that people within the Church just miss it sometimes. It was easy to take what I had been taught to believe, hold it up like an x-ray against the muddied light of broken people, and say, "Ah, see. I knew there were cracks in this belief system, and the people right here (points to x-ray) are proving it."

When you don't seem to fit into an environment, it's sometimes easier just to believe that you don't belong in that environment; that's how I felt during my whole upbringing in the Church. I was always someone who wasn't afraid to ask questions, to doubt what didn't seem right, to ask for explanations, and to not immediately give respect and honor just because "that's what you're supposed to do." These characteristics got me into a bit of trouble and caused adults to believe me to be, and then inform me that I was, rebellious. In hindsight, I know that what was seen as rebellion was my genuine desire for understanding. When I asked "Why?", I was made to feel like even the question suggested my intent to rebel, but that wasn't the case. I've always sought understanding of why things are the way they are. If there's a belief or a right or wrong way to do something, I want to understand why. If I hear a clear explanation to my question, it's not my heart to trash logic and continue to do my own thing. I actually want to know.

As you can imagine, that curiosity doesn't go over well in insecure environments. I define an *insecure environment* as one where those in positions of leadership feel as though their keeping or growing in position or influence is determined by their own ability to hold onto power. This atmosphere is unhealthy. When leadership is more concerned about making you feel wrong than they are about leading rightly, problems ensue.

I do not hold any bit of bitterness over the church leaders I grew up with because they did the best they could; however, I would like to encourage the next group of leaders to lead differently. If I could save someone else from feeling the condemnation and filth I did growing up, I would be quite honored.

Let me be clear when I say, I love the Church and all the beautiful people in it. I'm just of the mind that loving and leading broken people can and should be done better. That's why we're all here, running around on earth at the same time. God knows the power that we have when we come together, see an issue, make a collective decision to do what needs to be done, and fix it.

For some reason, I grew up with a serious distrust of authority. I think a few early, memorable experiences of injustice or just plain ole hurt surely helped develop my cynical outlook on anyone with a title or authority role in my life. I realized quickly that no one seemed to be a big fan of my questions ... and honestly, I don't blame them. There are few things more frustrating than being asked to explain something you're not equipped to explain; likewise, there are few things more infuriating than asking a question you really want to understand and not having it explained well. For instance, I was told on several occasions, "Young men don't talk like that. Young men don't dance like that. Young men don't walk or hold their arms like that." Now I don't hold any one person responsible for not being able to answer my, "But why?" questions when these statements would come up. I didn't receive these statements or the downward gaze and questioning glances that accompanied them from just one source. It was everyone from my elementary school P.E. teachers, to youth leaders, to pastors, to family members. Now, nearly thirty years later, I can look back and easily forgive these people with a, "They didn't know any better." The truth is they didn't.

Now let me say that forgiveness was not an easy place for me to reach. I've finally gotten to where I can mentally release my hands from around the necks of those who I had been angry with, but it was only after years of seeing how my own resentment and anger were not keeping anyone stuck but myself. I began believing that my characteristics (the things about me that just were) were inherently wrong and dirty. Believing I was dirty, I received every question about my characteristics as another judgment over me. I went from a bubbly toddler, who was famous for spinning my pacifier incredibly fast like it was a propeller, to a wounded young man, unable to express my hurt, much less deal with it.

I know that as much as I wanted to believe in Jesus growing up and as much as I wanted my faith to match up with the seemingly invincible nature of my parents' faith, I had a lot of circumstantial evidence that seemed to prove otherwise. To be honest, I just didn't think people in the Church were nice ... and, depending on who I meet on a given day, I might still think Christians suck at being nice. Hey, listen, I'm quite capable of wrongly ascribing an individual person's character to a whole group. But I'm sure I'm not the only one who does that, right?

I would hear the adults around me sing about the goodness and kindness of God and listen to a pastor talk about how much he loved us and believed in us as a congregation. Meanwhile, I would flashback in my mind to a few weeks prior when I overheard that same pastor talking about how much he disliked kids, specifically my age group. I was probably 13 at the time, so, I mean, I get it. But I just remember standing in the congregation when the pastor preached and thinking, *Liar.* If I knew Jesus then like I know Him now, a comment like that would probably make me laugh. But I didn't know Jesus back then, and my chubby-little-indignant-self added those innocuous but reckless comments to my stack of evidence against surrendering to Christ.

When I thought of my own view of the Lord, oftentimes the people whose voices loomed loudest in my head weren't those of my parents. I don't know if you're like me, but I was absolutely that kid who listened to any and every other adult around me except my parents. I know this drove them absolutely bonkers, and I don't blame them. I remember in high school my parents would tell me things that I would fight tooth and nail against. Then I would have one friend or mentor agree with what my parents said, and suddenly my mind was changed.

The variety of "Oh so NOW you believe us?!" looks I got from them were pretty classic. I steal a lot of those facial expressions now and use them when needed.

I was quick to find reasons to disprove the faith I saw in my parents by cross-referencing it with what I had seen in others. This whole "cycle of brokenness" thing is real. I had a dizzy amount of backseat comments on the way home from church about the pastors who seemed to care a great deal about being in charge but not so much about people. When I would hear my parents gently and kindly telling me to guard against judging others, I would roll my eyes and think, *Do my parents not see how crazy and inauthentic these people are? These people are just rude!* I'm sure I didn't know what "inauthentic" meant back then, but you get the point. If I could shake my pre-teen self, I would. I was so stinking judgmental of Christians at every turn because I was working through my own doubts. If I could disprove Jesus in the lives of those around me, then I wouldn't be held accountable for what I already knew to be true.

I had it completely backwards before I surrendered to Jesus. Instead of using the faults of others to disprove faith, I wish I'd had the wherewithal to use faith to disprove the faults of others. I would have been able to see, "Oh, that person just acted like a fool. But that's not who they are. Jesus says that person isn't a lost cause. They're rude right now, but Jesus is going to love on them. What that pastor just said cut me like a knife, but that's not his heart. I know he loves this church and the people in it." But, in my 13-year-old mind, grace didn't quite compute.

Being an extravert, a people person, and someone who doesn't mind attention, I quickly found myself getting involved in whatever drama-based activity I could find at my church. I did quite a few Sunday school sketches, human videos (oh yeah), plays, musicals, and everything in between. The problem was this put me directly under the authority of the very leaders and pastors who I had seen as incredibly flawed people, the people responsible for wounding me. In hindsight, it's clear I allowed one wound to lead way to and open the door for other wounds. I wasn't looking to find the good; I was looking to disprove goodness with the evidence of fallibility. This is a dangerous path to walk down and one I highly recommend you avoid at all cost. One person would say some joke that today I would laugh at, but back then it would send me into a tizzy. Then the next time I would see that person, I wouldn't be able to wear the pretense of kindness. I would disengage altogether.

Little known fact: I didn't go to youth camps as a child not because I wasn't allowed to, or because my parents didn't want me to go; I didn't go to youth camps because I had no desire to be left in the company of a bunch of people I didn't trust and who I didn't think cared about me. How's that for some real talk? Do we see how far those old hurts can carry us if we let them? They carried me way too far, and I began to rob myself of enjoying people altogether. Every weird church leadership thing I experienced, I would then add to the pile of disappointments. Every new friend I had would have to pay for the mistakes of the friends who went before them. I quickly saw how miserable this disillusionment was making me.

Expecting to be hurt is a surefire way of getting hurt.

People will let us down. But that doesn't change how we're supposed to love or what we're supposed to believe. Church will let us down because it is filled with flawed people who have been hurt and who hurt others. It's what we do as humans. We fall short. If I had known then that I could've found the perfect love and flawless relationship I was so desperate for in the person of Christ, I would've stopped being upset when people fell short of loving me and others perfectly. It would be as silly as if I became jealous of someone at a carnival while I was at Disney World staying at the Boardwalk Inn. (My favorite hotel in Disney World. We don't have to get into it, but my obsession with Disney Parks is real and probably unhealthy.) I would have zero reason to be jealous or disappointed that I'm not invited to the carnival when

I'm in the middle of Disney World. And yes, I did, in some way, just compare Disney World to a relationship with Jesus.

For a good chunk of my life, I looked for emotional and relational fulfillment from the people around me, to no avail. Surprise, surprise, more times than not I ended up wildly hurt and offended. Then I would end up spiraling into some depth of depression for a few days until Jesus would gently ask me, "Why does it bother you so much that x-person did or didn't do y-thing?" My response normally would go back to some disappointed expectation. I had expected "x-person" to love and care for me, and they had failed.

Jesus has always been so quick and kind in tone to say, "Right, but do you think I love you purely and care for you the way you need to be loved?" This is the point where I would normally start bawling and respond with, "Oh, I *know* you do." Then He'd add, "Good. So, can we go back to where I'm responsible for loving you the way you need to be loved and where you're responsible for loving others free of expectation?" In a single question, God would call out my idols, self-pity, hopelessness, and overall unhealthy expectations. But God's conviction never felt condemning. Even to this day, when He corrects me, it is always in the same kindness.

If you don't do life with Jesus yet, that's okay, but I have to tell you that I'm quite serious about His goodness. He isn't the teacher you had who humiliated you in high school. He's not the pastor who threw your sin out on a glass table for everyone to see at all angles. He isn't the coach you had that squashed your dreams. He isn't some moral dictator who is waiting to make you pay for your shortcomings. He isn't the parent who was always frustrated with you. He isn't the sibling who told you that you were embarrassing. Jesus is the Source of Kindness and Mercy. Even when He asks you to change course, it's never shouted from a mountaintop down to the valley where you are. He is not belittling. He comes down to your eye level, connects with you, and then gently lifts you to your feet.[48]

When He comes to check me on something within myself, Christ's correction is never spoken down to me as much as it's posed in the way of two friends on the couch talking about life. And yes, that's the truth. I'm a bit more sensitive than I normally let on, and I need soft gloves when it comes to dealing with my heart. Jesus, being Jesus, always meets me with the exact kindness I need, even in His correction. I wonder what would happen if we met a person with kindness first, instead of a frying pan of judgment to the head.

I'm grateful to know now that I no longer have to feel let down by the inconsistency of people because I have placed my trust wholly in Jesus. He doesn't let me down, and He won't. Despite what I may feel, Jesus is relentlessly good. He allows me to be "the failing friend" because He is the only Friend who never fails.[49] Jesus never turns His back on me when I act-a-fool. When I stray and misplace my focus, His kindness brings me back to repentance, which reveals even more of His goodness. When we're freed up to love without expectation, we get to experience greater relationship and intimacy with people as a by-product.

In turn, it's important to note that those who are constantly looking for people to be Jesus to them will not only rob themselves of right relationship with God but right relationship with people. We would never say this. We would just infer it with phrases like, "I wish you would show up for me." If you disagree, wait till the one reliable friend you have isn't so reliable. Wait until what's important to you doesn't register with the same importance to them. Wait till the one friend who knows you're "going through it" doesn't reach out to you for a month. Misplaced expectation kills: short and sweet.

With this issue noted, I'm so grateful for the heritage of faith I have in my parents. They've set me up to win in life, and I don't take that for granted. I wish I'd known that fact when I was gently made to be in church on Sunday morning and in youth group on Wednesday. Growing up, I didn't see this heritage of faith for the gift that it was. I really have had great models of what loving Jesus looks like; however, I was never quite content with letting their faith be mine. And, although I tried growing up to get it, I was at odds with myself and felt at odds with all things Church ... which led me to believe I was at odds with God.

In all honesty, I never felt fully wanted in the Church. Real talk. I realize that's a lot of "I feel" and could come across as a "Woe is me!" statement. I only share this because I know that a lot of people feel this way. Church wasn't a place that got me excited about much of anything outside of the fact that I knew we had to go to church before lunch. The "where" of lunch was really my main concern on Sunday mornings.

More than anything, church was a place where things didn't add up to me. It was a place where people talked about sin more than they talked about Jesus. It was a place where people believed the worst about me before believing the best. It was a place that was quick to uncover and shine a spotlight on my inadequacies and struggles. It was a place that spoke a lot over my life and not always in the best sense. I can even remember back to the summer before my 4th-grade year when I became very aware of this fact.

My family was hosting a party for our youth group at our house, and it was meant to be a welcome party for those moving up into middle school and high school. Now I was only in 4th grade, but I had a friend who was two years older than me. This group event was right after *NSYNC had released *"Bye Bye Bye."* Classic song. Amazing album. Don't come for me. But this was back when music videos were huge, and everyone was trying to learn choreography for their favorite songs.

So, this Saturday afternoon was no different, and I asked my friend (a girl) to join me in my room for a listening party/choreography rehearsal. We went upstairs, and I remember shutting my bedroom door as to not disrupt the party downstairs. We began playing the first couple of tracks. Within a few minutes, the youth pastor's wife was barging through my door. She immediately started in with, "What on earth are you two doing up here?" As a fourth grader, I was mortified. She asked why the door was shut, and, when I tried to explain, she didn't believe me. She told us both that we had sexual intentions with each other, without being so specific. She said that I wasn't being honest. She ordered us to immediately come downstairs. I remember looking at my friend as she slowly started walking toward the door. As this woman looked at me in the doorway of my room, I said a version of, "This is my house, and I'm not coming downstairs with you." My little bowed up fourth grade self was doing all he could to hold onto a shred of dignity, and that one little sentence was all I could muster up. I probably said it with tears in my eyes and a shaky voice because that's what normally happens when I'm angry and hurt to the core.

There wasn't any desire in my heart to do anything weird, sexual, or inappropriate with my friend. I wanted to listen to *NSYNC and to polish up some solid *Bye Bye Bye* choreography. But that day I was told by a person in authority, in the way I was addressed and treated, that I was dirty.

Now this story isn't something I share to place any bit of condemnation on the woman who, probably having experienced other craziness as a youth pastor's wife, was reacting to a situation she thought she knew. But the way we speak to children matters. What we believe about their intentions and who they are matters. The moments we think that are small and miniscule stick in the back of their minds. What we collect about ourselves in understanding who we are, in large part, comes from the adults who speak into our lives. Our identity is often shaped and molded at the hands of well-meaning people who don't have enough sense to think before they speak. This is not a new thing, and I'm sure my parents as well as theirs would have similar stories. But we've got to stop. Be kind and gentle with the kids you're around. They remember how you feel about them. When the youth pastor's wife accused me of perverse intentions, something shifted in me, partly because I let it and partly because the words spoken to me carried weight.

I've long since forgiven her and moved on, but that day my outlook and the way I felt about myself shifted. I was in fourth grade, and my home, that had been a safe place, was defiled in a way by someone who didn't know me or my heart, and who took to making inaccurate assumptions about who I was. I can't be upset with her though because this is what we do every day. I know it's something I do. We lay our experience as an interpretive grid over everyone we meet. Our experience grid colors our interpretation like stained glass. Then, regardless of who people really are, what we see are the same hues and colors we've seen elsewhere. We see the same disappointment or the same irritating selfishness. Since we carry a wallet-sized history book of hurt with us, no one ever gets a clean slate. This defense mechanism is no defense at all. In fact, I'd like to call it an offense mechanism. This is the way we make sure we get offended the way we expect to be offended so that we're not surprised or let down. If I feel like I already know who someone is based off one comment they made or how they let me down in whatever whack expectation I had, I immediately begin to cross reference the perceived hurt with past hurt. If I feel like I've been hurt the same way in the past, I immediately put all the unresolved hurt onto the shoulders of the person presently before me. Am I alone on this?

Sometimes it feels good and relieving to make someone pay for what you felt like was never actually resolved. We go through life and try to forgive those who have wronged us and who seemingly got away with it, but we sometimes quietly look for a moment of vindication. We silently hope that, at some point, we'll be the ones standing up saying, "See, I told you exactly what they were like, and no one believed me. I'll take my apology now!"

Maybe you've never had those thoughts or wanted that to happen. Maybe you're someone who can be wronged and not fazed. If that's you, you have 100% of my respect because you have mastered something I have not. I'd like to say that I can experience the fallibility of leaders and forgive as easily as I'd like to, but that's not always the case. Most of the time, I am crushed, then hurt, then angry ... and, if

I get to angry and don't pull the hurt from my heart, my anger turns into bitterness.

Now that tendency toward bitterness is insidious. Being crushed by an unfortunate situation is completely normal. Being hurt is understandable. But when we move over into bitterness, we've crossed into unholy land. We've almost made bitterness something we laugh at or minimize by saying, "Well, he's a bit bitter right now ... but he'll get over it." We tend to speak of bitterness is if it's a cold that leaves the body after a few days. Bitterness does not work like that. Bitterness doesn't just leave; in fact, it takes up residence and makes a home in the person who doesn't deal with it head on. Once bitterness sets up shop in a person, it then turns to resentment, and resentment is a dangerous thing. Let's be clear, I'm not talking about the kind of anger that leads us to righteously address unhealth.

God tells us to deal with unhealthy anger immediately.[50] Once the sun goes down and anger has time to ruminate in our bodies and minds, it can easily become bitterness, and then grow into resentment, which of course ends up as calcified unforgiveness. Deal with your bitterness promptly, or it, and the resentment and unforgiveness to follow, will act like quicksand for your mind and heart.

Just so you know, you're not alone if you have to fight hard against dark thoughts of hurt and resentment. So often I feel isolated and alone in the tormenting thoughts I have, but I'm not alone ... and neither are you.

It may be embarrassing to talk about, but of course as humans we have an innate desire to be right because we were designed to be right. I don't mean "right" as in an argument. We were meant to be in right relationship with right motives and right ways of being. In this "right" way of being, there would be no need to be defended or defend oneself. We wouldn't need to *feel like we are right* in a situation because *we would already be right in and of ourselves.* That was part of the original design in the Garden of Eden before Adam and Eve sinned by eating from the Tree of the Knowledge of Good and Evil. So now, because sin is on the scene, and the DNA of our desire to be right hasn't gone away, what do we do with it?

We cannot make ourselves right. That's why we fight, argue, and contend for our own character to be known and for others to believe the best about us at all points. But we are not capable of justifying ourselves when our character is maligned, attacked, or thought of poorly. We are not meant to be our own defense attorneys. Until we realize that we can never be right or properly defended against the wounds of a broken world apart from Jesus, we will stay stuck in the striving to do it ourselves, on our own.

When we take on the role of justice-seeker or righter-of-wrongs in our own lives, we can get a bit out of whack. I've made a lot of leaders pay for that one day that seemed to take me out. I've made my own parents suffer at the hand of my trust broken with other leaders. However, what grieves me the most is that I've done the exact same thing to God. Where others have hurt me without repentance, I have held Him accountable. Where I have felt let down and spat on, I have ascribed that to His account. I have cheated myself out of years of knowing Jesus for who He really is because I've demanded a payment for hurt He never caused.

There is no end to the cycle of hurt when every person we encounter is paying for the mistakes of the person who came before them. There has to be a finality to hurt, right? I mean, if there isn't, then what's the point? Someone must pay. Someone must make it right. Unhealed hurt looks like a lot of different things, and I'd venture to say, we all carry a little bit of it in our back pocket.

But what if someone was able to truly understand you while also seeing the fullness of your hurt? Not only that, what if someone were willing to make payment for the wrongs of others and even your wrongs by giving Himself as currency?

God, knowing that there must be payment for hurts, sufferings, and the wrongdoings of people, sent His more-than-willing Son. Jesus absorbed and took the penalty for sin and the hurt it causes on the cross. He received the wrath deserved for those who have hurt me, those I've hurt (Lord knows there's a lot), and my sin. He settled the score. When we choose Him, we get to hand over the hurt and He, willing and able to heal us, does just that. Jesus' heart has always been to break down the barriers between the Father and us and between us and others. Jesus' finished work on the cross is simultaneously the ultimate connector and wall breaker. What's even more beautiful is that Jesus went through the torment of humiliation and excruciating pain just so that it would be possible for Him to know you and me personally, as genuine friends. He did it all for the simple aim of having genuine and real friendship with us. Now the only thing left is to believe that His sacrifice is sufficient for our justification.

Once we believe it, then we start to live in such a way that reflects our trust in Christ and His finished work. It looks like the light of Christ transforming every part of us that used to be in darkness. I'll use myself as a guinea pig as we talk about what sanctification may look like, what it absolutely doesn't look like, and what I believe it can look like. I know *sanctification* may sound like a scary word, but it's really not. Sanctification is the process whereby people gradually come to desire holiness and act like Jesus. Sanctification means we begin to look more like Jesus than who we were before He rescued us.

I tend to love hard, and, when I go into a friendship with someone, it tends to be with the intention of that friendship lasting until one or both of us ends up in the ground. I play for keeps. Because of this side of me, I fight hard to not be wounded and hurt by those I love the most ... and I'll tell you, it's quite difficult for me. It's difficult for me to forgive. It's difficult for me to not be crushed. It's difficult for me to not defend myself.

One hard lesson I had to learn was when one of my nearest and dearest friends started dating a new person. My friend and I had walked years together and shared a great and quite intimate friendship. When the new relationship started, I was vocal and blunt about not immediately supporting my friend's interest in this new romantic venture. Over the course of the next couple of months, I watched our friendship deteriorate. I saw myself being shut out of her life. New, seemingly supportive friends appeared to take my place and enjoyed the intimate friendship with this person that I had lost. I went from inner-circle level with my friend to "See ya when I see ya." Man, it hurt.

As a result, I became incredibly angry. I felt as though my years of investment, of pouring out my heart while being a safe and steady listening ear, had been discarded. I then started looking back on the relationship and making a lot of character judgments of my own. That's what we do isn't it? When we are hurt by someone, we try to make it okay somehow, so we tear down the other person until we cannot logically make sense of missing them or of being in a relational position where we need them.

My friend got married, and we went a couple of years just not really speaking. I would see her and her spouse and immediately feel rejection. In my anger, I judged my friend and assumed she had beliefs about me and my intentions that weren't true. My anger seemed to ferment and become more toxic. Many people can look at this story and go, "Oh wow! This kid's intense. Can't imagine what it's like dealing with him and his emotions." To that I would say, yeah, it's a real treat. My friends have had this great privilege for quite some time, and those who have weathered the storm deserve medals.

As I look back at that isolated relationship, I can now see the Lord was just moving my friend and me in different directions to accomplish new things in both our lives. It was nothing more and nothing less. Although there was great hurt, God used it to sanctify me and cause me to lean on Him.

Think back to the last disagreement you had with a friend or the last time you didn't feel as close to someone as you thought you were. How did it impact your day-to-day life? I ask because, when I'm healthy and walking in daily relationship with the Lord, I can have disagreements or go through frustrating seasons with friends and still be fine. I don't become distraught or bothered by human fallibility. When I've chosen to make someone's view of me more important than God's view of me, life becomes quite messy. When I'm not healthy and not spending daily time with the Lord, I can be destroyed by a problem within a relationship. If a friend who I've invested a lot into doesn't return a call or respond in a way I think appropriate, I then take whatever I'm feeling as a judgment over myself. I understand the joy a friendship can bring into one's life, but we're not meant to be identified by it.

My friendship with the person who got married began right around the time I became a Christian. Jesus gave me incredible joy, new wisdom, and a peace that was attractive to others. Over the course of a few years, I began to take on the role of a confidant, at times advisor, at times corrector, at times class clown in a few people's lives. Without my even knowing it, I began to find my value in the fact that I was valuable to others. I was someone who was wanted at dinners and who became integral to hangs. As soon as my value became based off how often the phone rang, I got mixed up. It's not a healthy place to be.

So, when I went through this friendship adjustment, it wasn't only my feelings that got hurt; my identity was shaken. It would then take the next two years for God to recalibrate and realign my understanding of who I was. I enjoy being a supportive friend. When I look back, I see that who I was in people's lives wasn't a ton different than it is now. Still, because I know who I am now, I am not made or broken by the approval of others because my identity is firmly rooted in Christ. Of course, I have insecure days, weeks, and months, as we all do. But I snap back to knowing that anyone can walk into or out of my life, and I will be okay. That was a hard lesson to learn, but I'm sure grateful I walked through it.

It wasn't until my friend reached out to me, out of the blue, and asked if I wanted to go on a weekend road trip that I realized what the real issue was. When I was asked, my internal monologue was, *Oh so now you want relationship? You want my friendship only when it's convenient for you. That's where I'm going to exist in your life? Nope. Not going to happen.* The Lord gently said to me in that moment the same thing I had heard Ryan ask me all those years ago, "Aren't you tired, Cav?"

I instantly realized I had been angry over the same hurt for two years. Then, as He often does, God gently reminded me who I was called to be. He reminded me that I didn't have the right to withhold forgiveness when I've soaked it up from Jesus so liberally and without pause. I realized that my hurt in the situation and my right to defend myself or to ask for relational reparation was at direct odds with the Gospel. If I believe I am made right by the person of Christ and who He says I am, I have to know He does the same thing for others.

When a person's heart is not considered, and mistakes are made, God's grace is alive and sufficient enough to cover both sides.

I intimately learned that day that forgiveness is a choice and has a distinct feeling. It's like the relaxing of muscles, the loosening of a clenched fist, and exhaling after a long-held breath, all at once. Forgiveness is the Gospel at work, and I could finally see its work in me. This is where I wanted to live from now on, no longer in the land of resentment and grudge-holding, but in the land where forgiveness is a lifestyle and joy its by-product.

I had been playing the role of judgment-giver and justice-seeker and look where it had gotten me: two years of hurt feelings and bitterness while my friend was just living her life. I had to decide then about what kind of person and friend I was going to be. I was either going to be the one who held onto offense and kept a tally of all the ways in which I'd been hurt, or I was going to be intentional about holding my hands as open as possible with people. I was either going to chain people to me with guilt, manipulation, sharp words, and domineering communication, or I was going to freely forgive. I am not any person's jailor or captor, and life and relationship move in ebbs and flows that hurt sometimes. More than that, relationships change, grow, and diminish in accordance to God's will. It's not for me to have any other perspective than gratitude. Instead of looking at the lost time or the ways in which I wasn't included as much as I used to be, I could have chosen to be grateful for all the amazing times I had with my friend. I could have chosen to look at our disagreement as a small piece of a much bigger puzzle, which is growing up.

Although I didn't go with my friend on that trip, God transformed my heart. I was able to forgive and let go in an instant. Not but a couple of weeks later, my friend, along with her spouse, came to LA and asked to take me to lunch. We went and spent hours in one of my favorite spots just talking about life, God, and all that was going on. I don't share this story to say, "And now we're best friends again. See how great that worked out?" The truth is we are not even remotely as close as we used to be, but now it's okay. It doesn't break me to say that. I enjoy seeing her when I get to, and we laugh, reminisce, and get excited about the future ahead of us. It's good because I let go of my need to defend myself, to be right, and to have the justification I thought made sense. I now have a sweet friendship that has zero pressure.

This kind of friendship is just as precious as the day-to-day in-the-nitty-gritty-with-you relationship. Friendships all serve a purpose and have a place in our lives if we'll get out of the way and choose to let God defend, reveal, and, more than that, let God heal what we can't heal on our own. I don't need to defend myself anymore because Christ has already and ultimately made me right, along with my friends. I get to put down my law books and take the scowl off my face. The price has been paid for me to have clear eyes, with a free disposition, and a heart that easily loves and freely forgives. Hurt doesn't have the final say ... Jesus, Love Himself, does![51]

Thank You, Lord, for forgiveness and its power in our lives. Thank You that we can receive and give it freely. We don't have to be the judge or juror over anyone's life. Even when we're hurt to the core, we can remember how much You've forgiven us. This remembrance supplies us with the forgiveness we need for those we encounter.

Father, I ask that You show the reader what Your forgiveness truly does to a heart.

Please speak to specific hearts and begin showing them the joy of freely giving away forgiveness and the greater joy of watching its seeds take root in the hearts of those we forgive.

6

This is going to require some patience on your end, but I believe in you.

Do you ever have those days when you just feel like the ultimate failure? It may be based off something that's so incredibly small and doesn't matter. How about this one: ever had an awkward social exchange with someone? (I can't believe I'm writing this down.) If I go in for the classic bro handshake hug, I will absolutely miss 9 times out of 10. Shame over this mistake will then force me to spend the remainder of whatever day I'm going through reliving that single awkward miss. I'm talking ... there are full on slow motion recap videos playing on a loop in my head. I cannot be the only one who does this? I mean, it's definitely a possibility. Who am I kidding?

What do you do when you put your foot in your mouth in front of someone? I'm talking about those fully embarrassing, cringe-worthy, go-immediately-into-hiding-because-you-feel-that-unsafe moments. Now as much as I want to forget these moments of stupidity and thoughtlessness, they tend to play over in my mind for a couple of days. During the first 24 hours after I make the mistake, I may think about the event several times. Dwelling on my shame will cause me to get a fraction of the sleep I need. The next day, I will think about the same stupid thing, but maybe just a few times less; however, because I'm sleep deprived and not on my A-game, I'll allow the thoughts to linger longer than they should. Usually, the cycle of a mistake made and its residency in my mind is a few days, depending on the severity. I may go to bed and still be mildly tormented by the carelessness of my own words as I try to sleep, but, eventually, I will sleep. The next day, I'll awake, and, as I do, I'll struggle to remember what was so important to keep me up the night before. With a grimace, I'll remember, *Oh yes, the stupid thing I said.* That's probably the last time I'll think of that chance foolish encounter on its own ... until I say something stupid again.

Isn't it remarkable the amount of horribleness you can remember the second you make a mistake? The second I put my foot in my mouth, I suddenly remember a slew of other things I've carelessly said and the damage I've done in the past. Then I look at the details and statistics of my own behavior and make a judgment about myself. Suddenly, the conversation with the devil begins, most of the time, with me thinking I'm talking to myself ... *See, this is JUST like that last time you couldn't keep your mouth shut. This is why you're not getting further in life. You just can't get it together.* Then, almost instantly, the internal monologue switches to a conversation, or even more accurately, an interrogation: *You're not even trustworthy with your words. How can you be trustworthy with people? You want to be trusted with hearts; but, in a second, you're willing to crush another's heart for the sake of something you want to say. This really all goes back to why you're not where you want to be. You've never been able to control yourself, Cavanaugh. You haven't been able to control what you do, what you think, how you feel. Controlling what you say is honestly the least of your worries. I know you're worried about not looking like a weirdo in this room of people because you're thinking about how you just made a complete fool of yourself, and you're right. You are a fool.* In what can be as quick as a few seconds, I have had a full-on match with and lost to the enemy.

This is one of the biggest lies we believe on a daily basis, and I'll call it the *Lie of Yesterday*. The *Lie of Yesterday* says because you messed up in x, y, or z yesterday, you are not able to experience the fullness of today. This lie will tell you things like, *Well, you're not yet fully sorry for what you did, so you don't get to enjoy today. You really didn't learn the lesson from your mistake, so why would you be trusted with anything good today? You weren't able to control your mouth last week and keep from saying that hurtful thing to your mother, so what makes you think you can today? You weren't able to say 'no' to the advances of that attractive person last month, so what makes you think tonight will be any different? You haven't been able to kick that addiction so far, so what makes you think today could be your day to change?* I could continue with the hypothetical, internal monologue most people have at one time or another.

The enemy's native language is a fusion of lies and accusations. Think about the devil as the unholy antithesis of Christ. The devil lies. Christ is the truth. The devil condemns. Christ rescues. Christ never lies, and He took the condemnation against our sin on Himself. Satan only lies, and he lies to condemn people. Christ died to free people from condemnation with the truth that He wants relationship with us.

If you're feeling crushed under something you can't carry on your own, this fact might shock you: Jesus knows exactly how you feel. A unique aspect about Christianity, distinct from other world religions, is the character of the God Christians worship. Jesus is the only God who suffers and dies to save people. Not only does Jesus die, but He also stumbles and falls on the way to His destiny. On His way to Calvary, Jesus fell under the weight of the cross and someone helped Him carry the cross. My point is this: You won't find any other god who understands you the way Jesus does. Jesus experienced the feeling of stumbling and being crushed, so He understands how you feel and has the power to carry your burdens.

The enemy wants you to believe God's ashamed of you. He doesn't want you to know Jesus already carried your shame.

Here's the truth: the devil knows that if he can keep us looking back to the failures of yesterday, we won't see the victories of today. If we continue to keep our heads down, walking in the same track of defeat and self-fulfilling prophecies, then we won't see God do something new in us. So much of our walk in life and with the Lord, has to do with what we choose to focus on and give our attention to. If we're continuing down yesterday's thought patterns because we think those are the only thought patterns we can have, we will continue walking in circles in the same sins and issues. Although we often carry the ramifications of our actions yesterday into today, our hope and ability to change is not defined by our actions. Our hope and ability to change is defined by the fact that God is the God who enters our chaos and brings order.[52] He does not wait until we've tidied our lives up enough or worked out our issues on our own before He accepts, renews, and transforms us.[53] God doesn't love a future version of us. God loves us now. Remember, those who think they don't have a need for grace never know how wonderful it truly is. My whole faith in Jesus is wrapped up in my knowing that I am incredibly imperfect and that, in my imperfection, Jesus' grace, healing power, strength, mercy, and redemption are made real to me.[54]

So how do we combat the *Lie of Yesterday* on a practical level? It's not as difficult as one would think. See, the devil will always give you a bit of truth with the lie he's peddling. So, the first part is to recognize his strategy. When he reminds you of where you've missed, you can simply say, "Yes, I did miss it there." "Yes, what I did in that situation was wrong." But here's the flip: In your imperfect humanity, always point to the humanity of Jesus and HIS perfection. Then you can respond to your enemy, "You're right. I really missed it yesterday. If my ability to walk in freedom today and receive grace was based on my own actions, I would be in trouble. BUT Jesus became fully human, lived up to the holy standard of perfection, and sacrificed His life so I could receive the reward of His goodness instead of the penalty for the lack of my own. So, you're right, I DID miss it, but Jesus didn't. So, I get to be free today because Jesus won my freedom for yesterday, today, tomorrow, and always." And then you add your best church praise and run around whatever room you're in. At least, that's what I do. But obviously it's preferential.

Here's something to remember, too, when combating the voice of the enemy. The devil has no real authority of his own and very limited power. The impact of his power is enhanced or diminished conditioned on our response. The way the enemy gets us to empower him in our lives is by tempting us to agree with or entertain what he says. This is why you'll think you're just having a few moments of being down on yourself, and then you'll suddenly go incredibly dark or despairing. That's because partnering with the enemy's accusations against you is like tugging at a loose thread; it rarely ends well.

That's why you'll be having a perfectly fine day, and then you'll have a flash of something bad you've done or said. You'll dwell on the memory for an extra second or two, and, before long, you're down a scary thought path thinking things you know are not original to you. Every time we stay in a dangerous thought pattern a second too long or invest in a demonic accusation against us, we empower the enemy to guide us further down darker paths. When we think the dark thoughts or negative emotions are ours, we are not discerning the difference between our thoughts and the enemy's accusations. That's when we begin to take on the identity of whatever lie we believe. When we empower lies in our lives by agreeing with them, we empower the enemy. That's why it's crucial for us to understand the truth, not to only hear it from the mouths of others, but to have an internal radar that's able to hear the barrage of thoughts and differentiate them ... separating truth from lies. God's desire for us to stay founded in the Word is, in part, because it breeds life and discernment in us. Being rooted in God's Word helps us discern God's voice, our thoughts, and the enemy's accusations.

We rarely even realize what we're doing when we start getting in our heads about our failures, but this is exactly what it looks like. It looks like taking a failure or isolated incident into our hands, examining and massaging it, and watching it grow in front of our eyes until our failure obscures our redemptive view of Jesus. This is because, left in our hands, our weaknesses only grow. However, placed into the hands of Jesus, our weaknesses are diminished and subsumed by Christ's strength. The battle is not to try and cut off the flow of damning thoughts which we will all, at one point or another, face. The battle is in discerning our thoughts and knowing in Whose hands our weaknesses ultimately rest. This is why, as quickly as a demonic accusation enters your mind, you must refute and then dump it: "No, Satan. I am not a, b, or c." "Now, Jesus, I'm handing this thought over to You before I hurt myself with it."

I believe there is some innate human bent in us that makes us feel like, if we beat ourselves up enough over a mistake or spend enough time reviewing the mistake and thinking on its horribleness, we will then somehow earn freedom from torment. If we just feel bad enough, maybe it will make up for whatever misguided, poorly thought-out, or just plain wrong thing we did. This idea is just religion at its core. In religion, what I do or don't do determines my merit with God. In Christianity, Christ takes the penalty for all my sins and gives me His own perfect merit. I'm perfect in the eyes of God because Jesus is perfect. The path of religion, where I punish myself with self-loathing in an attempt to restore some merit with God, is just an incredibly passive form of penance. It's making me feel the weight of my own sin via the weight of my own thoughts. It's a warped way of trying to play god. Remember, we're not our own gods and have never been given the jurisdiction to think we are. Let's be honest: I've yet to meet a person who has found relief from drowning in guilt.

Giving over our thoughts to the Lord is yet another place in which we are called to relinquish our rights, even our right to what we believe about ourselves. We must give up our right to play god in our own lives and in the lives of others so that God can be God in our lives. Due to His goodness, God's desire for us to give up control isn't because He needs something from us. God doesn't need us to agree with His being God for Him to feel confident enough to move in our lives. God doesn't need human affirmation or acknowledgment to feel okay or validated. That's a human thing. To suggest that God's motive in asking us to do anything is actually for His own improvement or peace of mind would be to suggest that God is fallible and not completely whole and self-sufficient in Himself. A person with an incorrect view of God would look at God's desire for us to submit our hearts and minds to Him as His need to control us. They might think back to an unhealthy relationship where they were made to feel controlled, and they then ascribe that experience to the character of God. Out of this accusation against God's character, they say, *Oh no, I'm not going through that again. You can't have all of me because I've given all of me before, and it bit me in the butt.*

God is asking for our thoughts because they are better in His hands, plain and simple. When we're in Him, walking according to His ways and in relationship with Him, we're in better hands, too. The heart of God in asking of us or requiring something of us is only ever for our good and His glory. That's the truth. When God is glorified, He does even more in our lives. So even His glorification ends up still serving and loving us.

God knows that until we give up our control, we'll never see the destiny HE has planned for us, the one that, if we could see from His perspective, we'd always prefer anyway. Until we give up our thoughts to Him, we will never have His thoughts for us. Until we surrender our unhealthy thought patterns and tendency to wallow in our own mistakes, we won't move past our insufficiencies to see how truly sufficient He is. And just another bonus, God knows that we'll make ourselves sick trying to control every avenue of our lives and that we'll be frustrated and angry with ourselves when we mess up. The sooner we realize we're not qualified or called to be the judge and jury of our life, the sooner we'll start seeing a new level of freedom in areas not previously known.

Do you need another witness? You don't have to take my word for it when I say this freedom is possible. One of my dearest friends is a woman named Leigh. We've done a lot of life together and share a unique bond with one another. She'll tell you a story that illustrates how these claims about freedom function in actual relationship, in this case, our relationship. Here's Leigh:

For several years now, Cavanaugh James has been one of my greatest friends. He knows the best and worst things about me, and he loves me with rare loyalty. I value his integrity, wit, and the strength I see in him as a person who is fully yielded to Christ. Cav and I share many affections in common, musical theatre included, but there's a shared reality that helps bind us together as intimate friends: we share and understand the other's struggle.

For most of my life, like Cav, I've struggled with same-sex attraction or the feeling that I was not wanted by the opposite sex. I'm an identical twin, so, growing up, people always compared me to my twin sister. I remember someone telling me as a preteen, "I know how to tell you girls apart. Your sister is the girly girl, and you're more like a boy." These comments identifying me as less feminine than my sister escalated when I became a teenager. Though I wanted to be pursued by boys, they didn't seem interested in me. When someone did show interest in me, it was usually a girl. As a Christian, I faced temptation, but I never acted on it. When I met Cavanaugh, I remember experiencing this almost instantaneous kindred spirit affection for him. In one of our first friendship conversations, we were talking about writing, and he suddenly stopped mid conversation. He looked straight at me and said, "I know, Leigh, and I know that you know about me. We both know, and it's okay." Though this response was cryptic, we both knew its meaning. He told me that he knew I struggled with the same thing he did, and he assured me he wasn't scared away or going anywhere. We were going to do life together as ride or die friends.

I remember one evening a few years ago, Cav and I went to the theatre to watch the musical, *Jekyll and Hyde*. We had a hoot of a time together watching a show about literal identity conflict. Then, when I got home that evening, I turned on my computer and saw an email from a woman I'd worked with for a while on a project. I'd asked her to give me feedback on the project, and she wrote the following response: "I've learned that I disagree with you on almost everything. I think it is unloving and intolerant of you to believe that Jesus Christ is the only true God. Further, I'm pretty sure you're a lesbian or are repressed. I can't imagine a man alive who would want to marry you. You'd make life misery for a husband."

I sat in front of my computer screen in complete shock. Not only was the response disrespectful, this person wrote what she wrote in order to wound me, and she'd put it in writing. I remember texting Cav and asking him to call me in the morning. At 6:00 A.M. the phone rang, and Cav said "hi" to me in a groggy voice. I told him what had happened. I'll never forget his response. He said, "Well, that's demonic. That's from Satan, Leigh. And, because it's from Satan, we know exactly what this letter is: it's a lie. When something is demonic, it's actually encouraging in a weird way because not a word of it is true. Listen to me, Leigh. We are going to get off the phone now, and I'm giving you ten minutes before I call you back. During those ten minutes, you are free to grieve about what happened. You can cry or do whatever you want to do to express your pain, but, after ten minutes, when I call you again, that's the last time you get to dwell on or play back the tape of what she wrote. This is a lie, and it feeds on the authority you give it to hurt you. The reason this lie about your sexual identity keeps coming up is because the enemy knows this lie hurts you. He knows you consistently give it authority to wound you, and he's not creative, so he keeps using it because he knows it works. When you stop giving this lie the power to wound you by letting lies define who you are, the enemy will stop this attack. He'll have to shift tactics because this lie doesn't work anymore. Your ten minutes start now."

As soon as he hung up, I cried a little, but, more than anything, I remember the sensation of being absolutely protected. For ten minutes, it was like I sat in God's hand and felt Him holding me in complete safety. I even remember laughing out loud for joy. All at once I saw reality for what it was. I laughed at the enemy for being so uncreative in his attack. I laughed because I didn't have to cry anymore about this same lie I'd let wound me for years. I was free, truly free. All that mattered was who Jesus was and who He said I was to Him. My identity in Christ was the only identity that mattered, the only one with identity-shaping power.

Then Cav called me back in exactly ten minutes and said, "Okay, we're done. Now let's talk about that musical last night." So, we talked about *Jekyll and Hyde*, laughed, figured out new stage blocking to improve the show, and said goodbye. In that moment, God used Cavanaugh to reach into the serpent's mouth, grab hold of its fangs, and rip them out. I haven't heard that specific lie about my identity since that moment. It stopped that day because God used my dear friend to fight for my freedom, speak truth over me, and protect me with the Gospel. Since that time, our friendship continues to grow and deepen in trust. It's an incredible gift for both of us to be known by and to know someone who shares the struggle and the hope we have in Christ. Cav continues to fight for my freedom, and I continue to fight for his. We help one another see the reality of Jesus in the midst of our feelings, temptations, and frustrations. I hope and pray everyone has such a friendship where they can mutually love one another into the arms of Christ. That's true friendship. That's real love. That's how Jesus defanged the snake in my life. He can do the same for you.

To walk in this freedom, as Leigh and I help one another to do, we must let go of the unhealthy system of thought that says we're not only what we think, but we're also the sum of what we do or don't do. We've been trained to believe that our freedom is tied to what we do. Culture says, "You want freedom? Work and work until you're in a job that finally pays you enough to where you feel like you can go wherever you want, buy whatever you want, and be with whomever you want ... that's freedom." In other ways, we've defined "freedom" to mean following impulse after impulse because it's our right. In short, we've been sold the lie that being in control of our own lives is true freedom. Think about the idiocy of that thought. Controlling my own life, deciding everything for myself, and doing what I want when I want is ultimate freedom? True freedom is not being held down by my own inadequacies, because I know that my inadequacies don't define me. God defines me. True freedom is knowing that I am constantly being directed, guided, and led by the Holy Spirit. There are going to be times, possibly even seasons, when I'm messing up royally; still, because I have laid down my right to be in control of my life or to be my life's judge and jury, I am constantly en route to my God-given destiny.[55]

I'm not saying I'm removed from personal responsibility for my choices. I don't believe in the Gospel so I can get away with being less than I could be because Jesus has it all covered. I don't live as though my actions don't matter because He's going to snap me into perfection at some point. Although there are consequences for actions and unhealthy decisions, my life is not defined by those consequences. A judgment over a thing I've done could be, "That was wrong." But that judgement over my action doesn't mean, "I am wrong." When I sin, I don't have to live in the condemnation of believing that because of what I've done, God will reject me. Again, He doesn't accept me because of what I've done or not done. Jesus accepts me because of what He's done. We can be right in Christ and wrong in an action.

Culture has a difficult time with this thinking. We like to take a wrong action, tie it to the person who did the action, and ascribe every bit of damnation and defamation to that person until they have been stripped down to a base and deplorable form. Oh, we don't do that? How quickly does it take us to condemn a person in the limelight who falls? How long does it take people in the Church to take a pastor's entire life's work and call it null and void because of a sin or wrong thing said or done? Be very careful when putting down the media's handling of political candidates or public figures because we do it to our own in the Church. At least in the media they don't tie someone's eternal worth and salvation to a person's mistake or sin; but we've done that. Excuse me, we do that.

I'm about to share more thoughts on freedom, but I do so with some hesitancy because of the possibility that I might be misunderstood. One can quickly go from being *grace-averse* to *grace-abusive*. God's so good that, even in the extremes of either side, He has grace. My prayer is that God would bring us to a healthy perspective on grace and freedom.

If you grew up in any kind of church environment, I'm sure you've heard about grace being compared to a safety net. Now, although this analogy may be helpful, I find it to only be part of the truth. Yes, grace is there to catch us when we, like a trapeze artist, miss the bar after attempting some feat. But grace is more than a safety net. Grace is the trapeze bar that propels and enables us to leap into the air. Grace is the ladder up to and the platform itself from which we jump. The grace that will catch you when you fall is the very same grace that allowed you to try in the first place. The safety net is not where we are supposed to get comfortable. We are not supposed to make our bed on the proverbial safety net of God's grace. We are supposed to take the grace experienced and allow it to empower us to get up and back on the trapeze to jump and swing and jump again.

Grace is the transportation to our purpose.

It's grace that gives you the courage to chase after the things of God. It's grace that allows you to make it to the end of that year in college when you want to quit. It's grace that gives you the confidence to nail that job interview, and it's grace, all the same, if you aren't given the job. Everything that God does and is in our lives is enmeshed in and inseparably tied to His gracious nature. The gift of grace is not something to abuse or to take for granted, but it is something to believe and receive with gratitude. Grace is for us to see, to partake of, to give freely, and to steward. Grace is a weighty thing for us to know well.

Lord, thank You for not loving us based on our performance. Thank You also for gifting us with purpose and destiny, not reliant on our ability to be perfect, but reliant on Your grace. Thank You that your grace for us doesn't change and that You are never waiting for us to "feel bad enough" before You forgive and empower us. You don't hold our failures in front of our faces, and You don't ask us or anyone else to condemn us. You wait patiently and eagerly for us to realize we're forgiven. Right now, Lord, please reveal the depths of Your forgiveness to every single person reading this chapter.

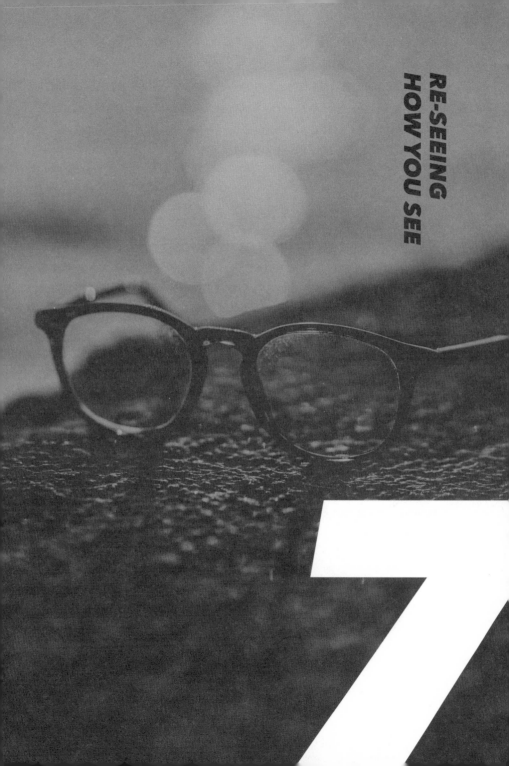

RE-SEEING
HOW YOU SEE

7

n this chapter, we're digging into *perception* and *perspective* and the importance of removing the spiritual cataracts from our eyes through the positioning of our perspective and perception. If we are to see God clearly, the way in which we see is crucial, and the vantage point from which we see, even more so.

Just to help differentiate the two terms, I like to think of *perspective* as the vantage point from which we see. *Perception* is how we interpret what we see and filter it into an opinion or belief.

Using myself as an example, I started having negative opinions about athletes because my *perspective* was from the place of a kid in high school who was bullied by a few of them. My *perception* was that all athletes were bad. Now, obviously, that's not true; however, my perspective helped form my perception. My former perception doesn't make the statement, "Athletes are bigoted, hateful, stupid, and self-centered," true. But we live in a culture where individual experiences are used to make relativistic truth claims. Our experiences are often far more involved in shaping our viewpoints than we'd maybe like to think. Just because our experiences can shape how we think, it doesn't make how we think correct. I have become enthralled by the notion that pure and unfiltered love can carry with it the power to transform because of its original source, Love Himself.

Have you ever gone back to listen to an outgoing answering machine message, heard yourself on a recording, or heard someone mimic how you sound? If you're like me, you respond with a, *Wait, THAT'S how I sound?* This may come as a surprise to you, but we never fully hear ourselves like others hear us. The way in which we say something often carries a tone, pitch, or affectation of which we are not aware.

I remember a crushing day. The event occurred where several of my lower moments have happened ... in the drive-thru line. That's real. I was probably 16 or 17, and I was going in for a quick sandwich, fries, and a coke. Everything about the moment was normal UNTIL the person I was giving my order to couldn't hear me. She responded, "I'm sorry, ma'am. What was the last thing you said?" Now, I realize that moment, taken by itself, could seem funny. But I cried for a while that night. And, to be honest, on the doorstep of being 30 years old, moments like this one still happen to me quite often. Only I don't shed tears over people thinking my voice sounds feminine anymore.

But that event at the drive-thru really hurt my heart. The devil knew exactly where to get me because he knew I had been making a conscious effort to lower my voice. The drive-thru attendant didn't hit on anything that was news to me. I was acutely aware of how I sounded to others and had begun to believe that I sounded like a woman myself.

You know how it feels when someone confirms something you're already struggling against? It was exactly that confirmation for me. After years of intermittent comments from well-meaning/careless people in and around my life, I started being intentional about lowering my voice and laugh, as much as possible, as to not draw extra attention to it. For a couple of weeks, I felt like I was killing it and doing a great job, you know, sounding like I'd gone through puberty. For the first time in a while, I felt confident in my new and lowered voice. I would even have little conversations with myself like, *I've got this. See? Just a little adjustment, a little change, and people are going to start seeing and thinking differently about me.* Then, when the drive-thru attendant didn't respond the way I thought she would, I was crushed. So instead of simply laughing it off, rolling my eyes, and moving on with my night, being mistaken for a girl stopped me in my tracks. I realized that what I had believed to be true about my own voice was immediately invalidated by the single response on the other side of the microphone. At this point in my life, I hadn't chosen Jesus, so my perception of truth was almost entirely based on the validation and approval of others.

My view of public perception and the inordinate value I put on the approval of others was toxic. In my mind, I was the sum of people's perceptions of me. You could hear that claim and think, *Well, yeah, Cav. That's kind of how it works.* But stick with me on this illustration. We're all, to a certain extent, the products of our environments, right? I don't mean to suggest that we fully become what and how we've been raised, but I do believe there are preferences, expectations, biases, opinions, and understandings of normalcy rooted in our upbringings.

Think about it. You may have grown up in a family where words were carefully counted, and, as a result, fights rarely happened. If someone from another family, where there wasn't much distance between what was thought and said, came over for dinner, they might be startled by how you live. It would be easy for the guest to make assumption that your family is emotionally closed off and doesn't communicate well based on the experience of communication in their home. Inversely, you could go over to your friend's house for dinner and make similar but contrasting assumptions and character judgments about their family. You might think your friend is reckless with their words. You might think their family is overly emotional or unhealthy in the way they communicate. The issue with both of your judgments would be that your standard of health and how a family should communicate is based solely off your own experiences and upbringings.

Despite what you perceive to be truly healthy or correct family functioning, there is an overarching fact that you might ignore: how you think people should or shouldn't be is how YOU think. If what you use to establish what is true about yourself, others, or a situation isn't based on a standard higher than your own experience and upbringing, you're taking on a role you were never meant to play.

How I gathered my initial perspective on my voice was based on a moving target. I had allowed the influence of countless people to tell me that there was something off about my voice, and I believed them. I listened to opinions from people who didn't know me from Adam and allowed those opinions to shape my perspective about myself. So, my perspective became just an echo of what was said to me by others.

Look at the cultural gravitational pull that's drawn my generation into a more self-focused and overly self-aware state. We are championed to hold onto our limited viewpoints and the high points of personality or character that seem to shine most brightly around us. We've heard the darkness that shouts loudest with phrases like, "Well, if that's your truth, that's your truth." Our perspective turns inward, and now we're back to playing god because what we've heard about ourselves from others, and believed in a moment of weakness, is now called "truth." Then we blindly think we've got a solid hold on what is true about ourselves. We couldn't be further from the truth. We hold onto a bunch of reverberations from a broken world and a collection of experiences in which our "truth" is validated. We think we have the whole picture, but we don't. This reality makes me sad. Truth is never meant to be informed by us; rather, we are meant to be informed by the Truth, Christ Jesus, and His perspective.

Here's the thing, I've lived in some pretty "progressive" cities in the country. Something I found especially hilarious in LA is that there is a real talk about energy. In the same city that champions an individual's right and ability to decide what is right for themselves, believing that those decisions only impact the individual making them, is also an incredible sensitivity to the energy of those same people. People talk so freely about the "vibe" of people and how they make a room feel. I have had countless conversations with my friends who don't follow Jesus who will pick up on, without even knowing it, the spiritual tone of a person. When I'm with Christian friends, and a person who sucks life out of a room comes around us, my friends or I might say, "Oh that person has some darkness on them," or "That person makes me uneasy. They've got company," or even, "That person is really struggling right now." We'll all pick up on it. When I'm with my friends who don't know Jesus or haven't made up their minds about who God is, they will see the same person, experience the same discomfort, but use different vocabulary to describe what they sense. Saying "energy" is less scary than acknowledging that there may be a very real enemy who sucks the life out of a room. I don't blame or condemn them for that language. I know if I hadn't chosen Jesus, I probably would be trying to explain away the same things the same way. I would absolutely say, "That person's vibe is crazy," or "I really don't like their energy," or "That person's aura is a horrible color right now" if I didn't follow Jesus. The reason two people can experience the same darkness in another person, or even in themselves, without ascribing it to the same source is that life and the struggles within an individual don't happen independent from the rest of the world.

The difference in responses is that the first person simply reacts to the struggling person's hurt or anger, while the person who loves Jesus sees through the hurt and anger to the spiritual source of the struggle. One response reacts. One response engages. What we believe about God and ourselves, we bring into every room into which we walk.[56]

We're told to not cross another's viewpoint in a negative way. Doing so would be to negate their perceived "truth." So, as not to offend another person, we'll even compromise or deny our own convictions. I intentionally put quotes around the word *truth*. See, without Jesus' perspective, what we really mean to say when we say, "truth" is "my perception of truth." I argue that if your perception of truth ends with your opinion, you're in a dangerous spot.

Feelings tend to be quite tricky and slithery things. They seem to morph and grow, occupying our minds and hearts with the force of primeval conquerors. They feel as real and concrete as truth, but feelings change in an instant. Truth does not. Feelings can make us believe falsehoods about others and ourselves with great conviction. They feel as close to us as our most founded beliefs yet tend to deceive us in insidious ways. Feelings will run your life if you allow them.

The truth? How I feel in any given moment has no part in defining God. I don't get to define God; God does. In this way, I stay in my lane ... which is usually the best lane. When I remind myself that His goodness is not determined by my present feelings or circumstances, I start to see His goodness all the more.

I'm not belittling feelings or emotions because I believe they serve a great purpose when paired with truth and conviction. They can be a great ally when they are ruled and not the ruler.

Any person in a lasting friendship, marriage, business partnership, etc. will tell you that feelings and emotions can't be the driving force behind anything. Feelings change and shift and, before long, will become discontent in any situation. If your emotions and feelings drive the way you love and do life with people, you will never see lasting relationships within your own life. Our roots must go deeper than the topsoil of how we feel. Nothing enduring grows in emotion alone. Affairs grow in our feelings. Short bursts of concentrated relationships grow in our emotions, but they soon die out with the change of seasons. If you want a lasting relationship with someone, there will be times you must choose to put your emotions and how you feel aside. If you want a lasting relationship with God, choose to submit and give your feelings over to Him and His goodness. It will be one of the healthiest decisions you've ever made.

Pause. This one is still especially difficult for me. I have been known to get lost in the sea of my own feelings and let them take over. By God's grace, I'm slowly but surely learning how to live above the undulation of emotions one can feel during any given day. Jesus has had to radically arrest my heart over and over and at deeper and deeper levels because I continue to be a bit hardheaded and blinded by my feelings at times. I've had to be made aware of my own need to stand on more than the quicksand of emotions for as long as I can remember.

When I finally decided that my emotions were no longer enough company for me, I had to surrender how I felt to what I knew. I knew that I was being called to more.[57] I knew that God was real. Now, I'm not talking about knowing God was real because I went to church and had parents who loved Jesus. I wasn't someone who readily accepted what I was told. Surprise, surprise.

I grew up being told about the goodness of God, but I experienced deep intense loneliness. So, I wrestled between the two "facts" of God's goodness and my loneliness. Succumbing to my emotions, I absolutely chose the readily available truth of how I felt over the quiet voice that I knew resonated in me. Let's be clear, I'm not talking about discovering God within myself. That is crazy, whack, and in no way true. We don't have Christ within us until we choose Him. The thinking that says, *We all have God inside ourselves, and we have to look within us to find divinity* is a shallow and blatant attempt to make gods of ourselves. I have no interest in being my own god, and, frankly, I have zero interest in you being god either.

Doing life with Jesus has not been exactly what I thought it would be. I don't know if it was my growing up around incredibly steady believers who had rock solid faith and seemed to have it all together, or if it was just some fantastic notion I built up in my head. Either way, I thought that turning my life over to Jesus and surrendering to His will would be like a perfect trade in. I give Him my old beat up Volkswagen, and He drives something around the corner for me that is sparkly and new with zero mileage. I was ready to trade in all of me to Jesus and to receive a full body transplant, complete with a new mind, struggle-free. Now, of course these aren't expectations I would've owned up to or even recognized in myself, but they were there. I was completely tired of myself and all the things I combatted on a daily basis, and, when the *Aha, it's Jesus I need* light turned on, I expected Him to just make me right. I know that sounds weird, but as anyone who has dealt with a sexuality-something would tell you, you spend so much time just feeling off and wrong within yourself; therefore, there's a real allure to all that struggle being made non-existent in an instant. Now I realize that my salvation was instantly secured and the final chapter of my story sealed when I invited Jesus into my heart, but the actual saving of me as a whole person was, and still is, a process. My relationship with process of any kind has been a love/hate one. I love what process establishes and the health it brings. I hate being in the thick of it.

My discontent with process created a litany of unhealthy and unful-filled expectations. I find that expectations, especially expectations we have about what we think the Lord should do, are the building blocks of the enemy's strongholds in our minds. Any time we manufacture ideas or expectations based off nothing more than our feelings, the way we assume life should be, we end up heading down a dangerous path. My own expectations, now that I look back and see their work in my life, have led me to a place where constant disappointments, like waves, repeatedly break against the foundation of my beliefs. I expected that in *getting saved*, as people say in the South, I would be immediately set right in all areas of my life, especially in my sexuality. I thought, from the moment of my acceptance of Christ, I would be free from same-sex attraction, tormenting thoughts, depression, habitual tendencies toward destructive behaviors, and anxiety about my life's purpose. I had hoped the man I saw when I looked in the mirror would be a complete stranger to my pre-Jesus struggles. Am I alone in this?

To be clear, I fully believe in having healthy expectations of the Lord. I also believe that, if we're not careful, our expectations can construct an inaccurate and skewed version of who God is. Self-centered expectations distort our perception of God. Through this lens, we tend to see Him as our divine butler who exists to do our bidding. In that perception, God is confined by our opinion of what He SHOULD be like or SHOULD be doing. Once in this dangerous territory, we start facing disappointment. In our fallibility and need to find a cause and culprit for our hurt, we blame God ... because He didn't live up to the constructs we made for Him. Our expectations of God should begin and end with His character and aligning our lives with the knowledge of His character. We should expect and trust what God says in His Word ... that He was, is, and will always be good. [58] We should expect Him to be for us and to be active in working for our good.[59] We should expect Him to be constant and never failing.[60]

Disappointment arises when we start to define the standard and job description we've created for God, whatever it may be. God's goodness in your life doesn't mean that He always answers your prayers the way you want Him to answer. His goodness means that He will answer. It may not be the way you thought or in the way you'd like, but His goodness in your life can't be changed by His failing to compromise who He is and how He answers your prayers to fit your human-designed version of a good God. If God and His relationship to you is dependent on how He meets your expectations of what He "should" do, then you have made yourself a god. When we do this, we create an idol we can bend to meet our will. When we've placed ourselves in the position of judging whether God has let us down, shown up the way we think He should, or fulfilled the requirements we see fit for a "good" God to fulfill, we are in the wrong and headed for an onslaught of disappointment. Once this disappointment is picked up by the devil, he uses our hurt to amplify the lies he tells us about God's character. The devil wants to turn our disappointment with God into doubts about His goodness. If we're disappointed in God, then we tend to begin to look for other things or people who are exactly what we expect, whether good or bad ... so that we're no longer disappointed. This is where expectation and the desire to control meet in the human heart. I believe this is where the enemy would want every person to end up. Because once you've decided God will let you down and that life in general lets you down, you begin to circle back to the unhealth you know and recognize. You may know that one person is going to let you down, break your heart, or use you, but it's easy to go back to him or her after a disappointment, because at least you know what you're in for. You may not say it out loud or have even recognized it in yourself before now, but your inner monologue would sound something like this:

- *Who cares if this guy/girl just wants to have sex and is using me? At least I know that's what they're about, and I won't be disappointed when it doesn't lead to a real relationship.*
- *Yeah, I know that playing the victim at every turn isolates me and causes people to not want to be around me, but then at least I won't be surprised when people walk away.*
- *I know that drug is only going to keep me distracted from my purpose, but it's better knowing I'm going to fail than to step out and be wrong.*
- *Yeah, I realize watching porn is incredibly unhealthy, but I'm never going to find someone who chooses me anyway, so what does it matter? It's better than waiting for someone who is probably not coming anyway.*

This is where the crosshairs of control and expectation take aim at your heart. We're flawed by nature; so by nature, when our expectations aren't met, we want answers. I said earlier that expectation, in a way, requires a culprit. By "culprit," I mean someone or something to blame if the expectation isn't met. The problem is that it doesn't end there. Expectation not only requires a culprit but a judgment over that culprit. So, when expectation isn't met, and your "culprit" is God, you think, *God doesn't care about my dreams. He fails me because He's not good to me. Putting my trust in Him is a sick joke.*

For my own life, I expected that I would put my faith in Christ and that, by merit of my doing so, He would instantly give me an attraction to the opposite sex. Because that didn't happen, my disappointment told me that I was wrong to not only expect that change but to expect God to be the one to heal my mind. Because He didn't answer me the way I wanted Him to or thought He should, I subconsciously started withdrawing my faith from God's account.

If you don't believe that this is something we do, let me ask you a question. Have you ever felt genuinely wronged or hurt by a friend? Unless you're a hermit choosing to live your life out in the woods some-where, I'm sure you've experienced hurt caused by people you love. Side bar, I've absolutely thought about that lifestyle at several points, so, if you're reading this book from your cabin, I get you. But also, come back to society. We miss you. I digress.

When someone hurts us, it causes us to recoil then withdraw, some-times for a short period of time, sometimes for a long one. We often say, "It felt like I was punched in the stomach" or "stabbed in the back." Both actions cause a natural movement away from the source of pain. If you hurt me physically, I will want to establish distance from you. If you hurt me emotionally, I will withdraw. The issue is what we do in our day-to-day lives is never too far from what we do with God. If you believe that God is capable of hurting you, because of the expectations and markers you've set up that He's failing to meet, you will in fact hold Him accountable for your hurt and react accordingly. Having searched for a safe place for your heart where you won't find disappointment, hurt, and rejection, you will eventually settle on the fact that you are the only person who is safe to be around. But the problem is that you will let yourself down. When you start to be hurt by your own thoughts and actions, what then? This is the aim of the enemy, for us to eventually be left alone with ourselves.

As I said in the first chapter, our own devices are killing us. When we are left to ourselves to be the gods of ourselves, we only hurt and diminish ourselves. The reason is, we buy into the lie that we're capable of doing what we need to do in our own strength. We believe that we can make ourselves good, happy, whole, or whatever positive thing we think we're able to work out ourselves. I mean, look at the world we live in today. The power of "I" is championed at every turn. We hear political leaders, celebrities, even our own friends boast about their self-made successes, how they're happiest alone, how they don't need anyone. Hate to break it to you, but no. That's code for, *I realized that I can't control anything or anyone but myself, and even that I'm not great at controlling. But I'm good enough to LOOK like I'm doing great by myself, so I'll settle for that.* That's just control masquerading as independence, and we celebrate it. I mean, maybe it's just me. Maybe I'm on my own in this, but I have tried to make myself happy, and I can't. I have tried to control my own actions apart from God's authority and based on my own will, and I fail every time. Maybe not all at once and maybe not immediately, but I eventually am left with the same brokenness and issues from which I initially sought to break free. I make a terrible savior for myself.

Our expectations are like a scaffolding framework constructed around who we think God is. The thing is,

God is much bigger than the borders of any human expectation.[61]

If we're not willing to let the framework fall, or, if necessary, pull it down, we will never see God for who He really is. We will only see shadows and recesses of His attributes skewed by our own sin-built, broken perceptions.

Our perception of God's goodness does not determine God's goodness in our lives. Our perspective has to shift. Because I know God is good and my expectation of Him and His character is that He's good, I don't get to be disappointed when He doesn't answer my prayer the way I think He ought to answer. Because His goodness is unchanging and my belief in that fact is sure, I then have to adjust my expectation around who I know Him to be. If He doesn't answer me the way I want Him to, that means my expectation is out of whack. I know He's perfect in all His ways. If I'm disappointed or feel disenfranchised from an aspect of His love or provision in my life, it's on me, not Him. If I feel disappointed, it's because I put my hope and expectation somewhere it doesn't belong. Just trust me because I've run the gamut of disappointed, to hurt, to withdrawal of my affections and love, to isolation and being my own god. Can I please just save you the trouble? The problem is never God. The issue is never that God didn't operate or love you the way He promised to love you. He will never fail to come through for you. He never leaves you. He never fails to provide for you. He never fails you in any way. If you're fighting disappointment in the Lord, it's because your expectations have been incorrect. Getting to a consistent and trusting relationship with the Lord means a surrendering of all expectations of how He should be and replacing them with the trust of knowing who He is.

I'm a restless person by nature. In fact, anyone who does any bit of life with me could tell you that I'm not the best at being patient. Well, I should say I'm not the best at being patient with my life to be exact. I went to Bible college wanting to lead worship, then got my degree in marketing from a university, then moved to New York to pursue acting, moved back home and took a job in social media, then went to LA for acting school, and came back to Texas to do a musical and write a book. On paper, I'm literally all over the place. My life looks like a random game of connect-the-dots. As much as I'd like to say I've given up the need to make it all make sense and have it all figured out, I'm not there yet. If I'm being honest, I would say that I loathe the way that sounds and looks. Even as I think about my progression, I can easily see the nearly ten years of my life gone. And, if I choose, I could be bombarded and made to struggle with my perceived failures. I know this isn't a new struggle or one that is unique to me, but I've spent a great deal of time just feeling restless because I've attached my ability to rest to whatever season I'm currently in.

My life has felt like a series of failed attempts at chasing after dreams, and then being brought back to "training camp," so to speak, with the Lord. You know training camp. It's that period in life where you're not where you want to be, not sure where you're going, and not sure how to get there ... mostly because there are things you're having to work out in yourself before the next part of your life can unfold. It's frustrating, tedious, and feels like your life has gone into slow motion. It's a helpful period and necessary to a point, but it's not usually the most exciting season. It feels like limbo, an in-between point, stuck-in-the-gray kind of place. As much as I'm grateful for the "training camp" seasons in life and see their value, this has been, and continues to be, a battle for me.

And just like that, feelings can even hijack the writing of a book. The last two paragraphs you read might be the most concise representation of how I've felt over the past several years. Even as I look over them, I want to grimace and say, "Well, yep. That's exactly how I feel." But remember, how I feel doesn't get to be god anymore.

I know God sees me. He alone knows the full trajectory of my life. I know He loves me. But again I "feel" like I've wasted so much time. I "feel" like a bullet that's missed its mark. God's the Marksmen, but right now I feel like I'm on the brink of spiraling. This is a choice we all encounter at one point or another: to spiral or not to spiral? ... *THAT is the question.* How we answer that question depends on our perspective and our willingness to let it change. I'm not willing to let my own vantage point be the determining factor in how I live my life and purpose.

See, God is going to accomplish in my life what He intends to accomplish. But if I'm not careful in moving my own expectations of how life should look or the dreams that were supposed to come true out of the way, then I've got a problem. When I hold to what I see, how I feel, or what I believe as truth more readily than what God deems as truth, I am trying to fit God's ways into my limited understanding. That never works out well.

Growing up, I had the real privilege of having grandparents on both sides with land in different parts of Texas. So many of my weekends were spent enjoying and exploring the country with my siblings, cousins, and friends. One of my closest friends to this day, my oldest friend period, is a great man called Sam. Our grandparents were even friends. Our dads had the same first name and were in the same nursery. They are still friends today. We absolutely grew up together, and Sam's family lived a mile down the road from my grandparents' place near Palestine, TX. When I came into town, Sam and I would almost immediately find ourselves out on a couple of four wheelers in the back parts and corners of the land seeing what new things we could find or areas we could explore. On this land, there was a little creek that we enjoyed exploring. One day we came upon some antique bikes and yard things that had been left for a few decades on the land. I remember coming up on a bike that was tied to a tree. We took it, convinced we could gussy it up and make a penny or two from it. We didn't. But then I remember seeing another bike. This one was a children's bike, and I could tell it was something beautiful in its day. This one wasn't where we could get to it because a tree had completely grown up through one of the spokes in the wheel. The bike was fused into the tree. I remember looking at it for probably a few seconds, just trying to understand how that could've happened. Now some 20 years later, as I try and understand more about the Lord, I see that picture in my head much differently. Our expectations and the ways we think are a lot like an antiquated bicycle we leave in the middle of the forest of our lives. And if we're not mindful, the dreams we were convinced of as a child, the ways we thought we'd be success-ful, even our expectations of people, can, much like an old bike with a tree grown through it, end up as rusted man-made thinking, frozen in a fight against the seed that turned to timber. I'll show you what this looks like in the natural. Ever have a friend who is experiencing a success, but they can't really enjoy it because it isn't quite the fulfill-ment of their expectation? I may have a great job, but if it's not my dream job, then God's let me down. I may have great opportunities, but, if they're not the ones I'm wanting, then they must not be right.

I could have the perfect wife in front of me, but because she may not be who I initially dreamt up, I miss recognizing her.

I just don't want to have my broken expectation caught up in any bit of God's destiny. I don't want His ways, plans, and ideals for my life to grow around what I refuse to let go of ... like a beautiful tree with a deteriorating and nonfunctional bike in the middle of its trunk.

God's Word is always the seed that will grow in your life that is most inconvenient to your perspective. For some people, their bike is to be married by 40. For other people, their bike may be a childhood dream. For others, it could be a failure they're unwilling to let go. Everyone has a different bike. And I know what you may be asking, "Why does he keep using this children's bike as a metaphor? What's the point?" I'll tell you the point. Your perspective of your own life is always going to be trash compared to what God's got dreamed up for you. So, ditch your old bike, and let God grow when, where, and what He wants in your life. Trust that what He's doing in your life, even if the timing seems slow and draining, is going to be better than anything you could do for yourself. Clear the forest floor of your heart and mind so there is nothing that will contend with what God's designed for your life.[62]

Lord, thank You for Your perspective and that we don't have to trust our own. I am so grateful how I see isn't the whole picture. I'm thankful my limited understanding isn't my god. You are.

So, I ask right now that You would reveal greater lines of sight to every reader. Please take their viewpoint and zoom out to show them a much fuller picture. Please reach down and remove any spiritual blinders or cataracts occluding the reader's view of You. Your viewpoint is the only one we need, Lord.

TO KNOW AND BE KNOWN

8

We are designed to know and be known, vulnerabilities and all. It's as original to us as the Garden of Eden. Think about it, when the Lord created Adam and Eve, there was nothing hidden between them. There were no secret desires that went unnoticed and no relational distance between them. Adam was the Lord's, and they were friends, so much so that the naming of every living thing, creature, plant, tree, or flower was left up to Adam. In fact, the Bible says the Lord created all the animals and then immediately brought them to Adam to see what HE would call them. Adam was a trusted friend of the Lord and one the Lord loved to empower, give creative authority to, and walk with side by side. THIS is our original design as human beings. I use that phrase "original design" because I'm not a fan of how many people in the Church have used it. This phrasing has been used to make men and women feel as though their sole original design was to have a healthy sexual relationship with spouses of the opposite sex ... But that is not our ORIGINAL design. Our original design is to be a friend of God. We're meant to be truly known and accessible partners with God. We're meant, before anything else, to be a trusted co-laborer working hand in hand with the Father in true intimacy. Before Adam wanted anything from God, i.e. a wife, he spent time doing life with God.

Sidebar — how long do you think it must've taken for him to name every creature? Genesis 2 tells us that before Adam realized he needed a helper, he had named every kind of livestock, bird, and beast of the field. Now I realize that it may seem like I'm harping on an insignificant fact, but I'm trying to point out that before man was having relationship with woman, he was spending time having relationship with God. I would venture to say that if we spent a little more time trying to intimately know the Lord before we dove into every relationship that came our way, we'd save ourselves a great deal of trouble. That's just a little freebie for you. If you're someone who has been in and out of failed relationships and feel as though you're cursed in the area of love, might I gently suggest there's a possibility you don't have an accurate view of healthy relationship. If you build your expectation of what's healthy and what makes sense in relationships based off your own ideals, the culture, brokenness in the people around you, Hollywood, or what you've been taught from your own experience, you may be out of process. Now this doesn't mean that you ought to feel condemned or put down for being out of process, because, I assure you, we have all been there. A good chunk of us are still there. Be that as it may, you will never be able to purely love and be loved by others without first knowing how to love and be loved by God. If you try to do so apart from God, you will be frustrated in your own strength and willpower. We were designed to first be filled by the pure and only true Source of love before we pour into another relationship.

God is the God of process. He knows that intimacy with people is important to us because He designed it to be important. God also knows that for you and I to truly be able to love others, we must first be loved by Him. I understand if this sounds like nonsense at first glance. You might be thinking, *Cavanaugh doesn't know what he's talking about. I've lived a lot more life, and his idea about first being intimate with the*

Lord is sweet, but naïve. May I suggest, if a part of you wants to bow up right now, it's probably because this is an area the enemy really doesn't want you to sort out. Sometimes, we tend to be more protective of our own stagnancy than we are invested in our own growth. It's a shame isn't it? Sometimes we would rather spend more time defending what's never brought actual health to us than we would to have a slightly uncomfortable conversation that leads to lasting, healthy change. But just so you know, the enemy tends to have a real issue with growth and change. He's a jerk that way. He knows the more we surrender ourselves to the knowledge of a loving and good Father, the less opportunity he has to lead us into stagnant, stuck, harmful places.

But for the sake of argument, let's have a quick conversation. We live in a society that is sex-positive, pro anything-you-want-to-do, and a champion of self-destructive but temporarily satisfying things. Of course, there are studies that tout the liberation of the sexual movement and how people are finally able to live as they truly want to live. The problem with that thinking is that few people are addressing the mental, spiritual, or emotional impact of being more focused on sexually gratifying encounters than legitimate relationships. No, no, no, we definitely don't want to discuss what promiscuity does to the psyche of someone, or how it changes the very nature and natural condition of a person. We say, "Well, if two consenting adults want to frolic as they choose, what concern of it is yours?" You see, this issue isn't really about sex. I mean, the thing is, you can tell a tree by its fruit. You can profess to be as healthy as you desire, but, regardless of what you say, your life and

overall disposition will tell more than your words ever do. It's no different than someone telling you they're a strong and independent man
or woman, just fine by themselves. Yet the need to verbally announce
one's strength and independence is often an attempt to mask insecurity
and frailty. If that loud-about-my-strength person doesn't feel sexually
attractive, wanted, emotionally supported, believed in, or empowered
to do exactly what they want, you will see that self-proclaimed strength
whither into the insecure "vine" it truly is.

When I say *vine*, I mean to say that it derives its strength and ability
to thrive and survive from the very support on which it depends. A vine
has no real strength of its own. A vine is only as strong as its support
system. In the same way, when your hope is dependent on others, you
have tried to grow your vine on a wonky and untrustworthy support
system. Why? People fail. That's why our support and dependence
must be founded in an unchanging and unwavering constant; otherwise, we never grow, climb, and eventually yield the healthy fruit we're
created to yield. When your identity, success, consistency, health, and
overall joy are tied to the inconsistency of a person, organization, job,
or anything other than Jesus, you lose.

When we're not wholly reliant on the unchanging One, we're closer
to having our support system uprooted by the next strong wind than
we are to feeling secure and confident. Our lives become inconsistent
and disorienting because we have placed security where it was never
meant to be placed. In fact, if a boyfriend or girlfriend broke your heart

years ago and you still find it hard to be just as genuinely happy and joyful as you were when you were with him or her, in love, let me warn: you might have made that relationship an idol and another person your functional god. Trusting a person or relationship to be the root system supporting your whole life ends in disappointment, anger, sorrow, and cynicism. People make terrible gods. And we wonder why people walk around so miserable and unfulfilled. You will never be fulfilled until you realize that you are whole and complete in Christ ... not in him or her.

You can sleep around all day long, doing whatever you desire, and tell me till you're blue in the face how liberated and happy you feel. I've been lied to before, and it wouldn't be the first time I cocked my head and said, "Oh yeah? Tell me more about that." I've surrendered my life to God, and He sees everything at all times.[63] He knows my heart is to know Him. I want to know others so that, in turn, I come to know Him better. It's a beautiful and ever-growing cycle of knowing Jesus, so I can know others, so I can know Him at a deeper level. I live in that space. Because of that cycle, it sometimes feels like I have emotional x-ray vision, as do many people who love and have surrendered to Jesus. No, of course we don't always show our hand or reveal what we see. Sometimes God reveals things to us about others that are simply meant to drive us to intercede on their behalf. Sometimes the insight the Lord gives us is not meant to be shared.

That's an actual word for someone. Just because you sense something, doesn't always mean you're supposed to say something. A word of knowledge spoken out of season or at a time not given by God can cause shame and uncovering as opposed to healing. Anytime we speak a spiritual insight to someone and do so when we want to, as opposed to when we're asked to by the Lord, we open ourselves up for that truth to be distorted and discarded. If God's not behind what you say, He's not going to protect the word itself or back it with authority and power. It's not worth losing a relationship just to say what you feel needs to be said, especially when God isn't directing you to say it. Stop, breathe, and ask the Lord if it's something God wants you to share. This will save you a lot of frustration and uncomfortable responses.

This warning noted, when we're tapped into what the Lord is doing and saying, we tend to be able to see into other's hearts. Sometimes we can even hear the record that is playing on a loop in their head. We might even know the lies that they've been told and continue to repeat.

If you're reading this with skepticism, I absolutely understand it, but try me ... or even better, come hang out with my friends and me for a bit. One of my first experiences of seeing into the hearts of others was probably about nine years ago. I was hanging with my friend, Ry, and we were eating some Mongolian food out on a patio one summer night ... because Mongolian is delicious. Need I say more? We were enjoying our dinner and making metaphors out of inanimate objects on the table while trying to top each other with hilarity, as friends should as far as I'm concerned. I would give you an example of what it looks like, but, if you've seen my

Instagram videos, I think you'll have a good idea of what this interaction looks like. But I digress.

We were eating and focused on each other, but then a woman slowly walked by our table wearing a full-length fur coat (in July). When she walked by, we both felt a tangible and demonic chill. We stopped mid-conversation and asked each other, "Did you feel that?" As soon as she left, Ry's eyes opened wide and he said, "She has company." I immediately knew he was talking about spiritual company. Now, if you ever hear me say, "Oh, I feel some company in the room," you'll know what I mean. It immediately changed the tone of our conversation and our overall levity. We went from laughing and being light to promptly getting out of the restaurant. It was as if spiritual famine, addiction, and brokenness itself walked by our table. At this point in my life, I would hopefully handle that situation much differently. Now I know I have authority over that darkness and that I could have, if I had been leaning into the voice of the Lord, addressed that darkness head on and won. But I was a baby believer and ran. I'm not proud of it, but I share that story to say that the devil would love nothing more than to tell you your gut feelings, your sensitivities, and "Spidey" senses are wrong and nothing more than emotional responses. But let's just go ahead and chalk that idea up to a lie. We are all born with and given, according to our willingness to continually grow and lean into our sensitivities, the ability to discern past someone's words into what's going on in their heart. I'm telling you, doing life with Jesus via the Holy Spirit is like being gifted with "a very particular set of skills." Why yes, yes, I did just spiritually compare myself to Liam Neeson in *Taken*. However, I know my authority now, and you shan't convince me otherwise.

You see what the world doesn't know is that those who have surrendered to Jesus are suddenly given and gradually trained in a network of communication and understanding that is hidden to the natural eye. This empowerment can make us quite emotionally intelligent and sensitive, and great teammates for each other. When I meet someone, I almost immediately know if they know the Lord. My "Spidey" senses begin to tingle when they talk, and it's like I'm immediately talking with someone who I know understands me. At several points I've been at a dinner with a big group of people, and I'll focus in on someone after a few minutes of listening to their conversation or seeing an overall brightness in their disposition. I'll not so casually ask something like, "You love Jesus, don't you?" I have about all the subtlety of a freight train sometimes, and that is equally true.

To save you some heartache, I'll level with you. I don't enjoy or have respect for the phrase "my truth," and I'll happily explain why. When you separate your truth from the universal standard of truth, you build an island of morality for yourself where you and your perception of truth reign supreme. The person who talks about truth as "my truth" implies that they can govern for themselves what is right and wrong. To put it another way, on the island of "you," you're independent from all others. Whatever is decided on your island affects your island and no other areas. But life simply doesn't happen in a vacuum, and our decisions, even internally made, affect the lives of others. It's lunacy to me that we don't see the hypocrisy in our society with the whole *live and let live* mantra we've taken to heart. The brain in my skull is about three pounds, and it often tries to tell me I'd make a better god than God. That's crazy. Looking back, the most miserable moments of my life all have one thing in common: I was trying to be the functional god in my life or trusting a person or thing to be god for me.

We are truly living in the middle of a culture which says, "You can do whatever you want and be with whomever you want as long as it makes you 'happy.'" This thinking makes me want to "lash out irrationally." Shout-out to *The Santa Clause* for giving me that gem of a phrase. The pursuit of happiness as an end in itself will leave a person dry and unsatisfied. That's because happiness is a transient emotion that comes and goes on a whim. When a child opens a gift on Christmas morning, they may be thrilled with the toy for a day, week, or year. But eventually, they need another toy to make them happy. Any activity or toy eventually gets boring. Have you ever wondered why there are so many bored people? My guess is it has something to do with people trying to find their ultimate joy in created stuff rather than their Creator. When the human heart worships a created thing, perversion happens. The created thing, as good as it may be, cannot bear the wait of the human desire to worship and will crumble under the hope that this thing or person will fulfill me. When the human heart worships Jesus, the Creator, our worship frees us up to enjoy created things, and people, without making them the place we source identity and purpose. Loving Jesus is the way to love anything or anyone rightly and well.

Let me say this before I go any further: I have no stone or bit of judgment to throw at anyone who has had an active sex life outside of marriage because, to be honest, I could just as easily live that way. I've seen too many people I love get their hearts broken because they gave their bodies and hearts to other people without the safety of real commitment in the covenant of marriage.

I'll tell you what I've learned just by observation, and you tell me if I'm wrong.

We live in a time where the phrase "daddy issues" has become so common that it's used by men and women alike to describe those who are "emotionally too much work" or "have problems" or are "too desperate for attention." It's also a celebrated pop culture theme. We've even gone so far as to merchandise the phrase and turn it into T-shirts, memes, Instagram accounts, coffee cups, and even TV shows. Many people look at someone and how they're struggling and attribute it to the way in which that person received or didn't receive love from their earthly father. Intimacy with God the Father affects every other intimacy we have. If you are not first taught what love looks like through experiencing the purest form of love in the Father, you'll look to every cheap knock off there is.

Just so we're clear, when I talk about intimacy, I'm not talking about sex, although that is a by-product of true and healthy intimacy. By intimacy, I'm talking about true familiarity, closeness, tenderness, affection, and confidence in a relationship with another person. God knows intimacy that is formed without Him in the center leads to destruction.

God wants to be in the center of who we are, what we do, and how we live in relationship with others. He knows that intimacy based on other ground than Him is shifting ground that can't sustain the weight that true intimacy is meant to bear.[64] The issue I take with sex outside of marriage has nothing to do with sex on its own. I'm pro sex. If you're married, have all the sex. The issue isn't with sex. It's just that sex was designed as an act meant to reinforce and model in the physical what we are doing in the spiritual when we give ourselves wholly to another person. Think about it. To get married, and to do so vulnerably, is to invite another person to see and experience every bit of oneself, good, bad, and ugly ... and to do so for the rest of your life. When we make that commitment, then the act of sex is used in right function to bring two people into more intimacy. We see another person's whole body, they see ours, and we still choose each other. That's a pretty intimate act. But because sex is designed to bring about more communion and closeness, when it is engaged in out of order, it can bring about the feeling of being known by someone, but that feeling has no foundation in the actual God-blessed union of marriage, so it turns to dysfunction. That's why a one-night stand can make young men and women believe they're in love. That's why hearts and friendships are broken when that line is crossed without the commitment covering it. That's why people have affairs, believe they've fallen in love, only to look up a couple years down the road to realize that they'd fallen in lust. Lust is great at looking like love at first glance. It can give you the same heart flutters, the same middle school feelings that we all remember, but once that lust gets what it seeks, which is usually sex, the lights come up, and the truth is seen; it was only lust. Also, if this is an area of struggle for you, just know there's hope for you. God can handle your struggle. He's not stressed about it either. But that's why we have to first choose intimacy with the Lord. That way we're not starving for it from people.

When we're not giving God the highest focus in our lives relationally, we end up accepting poor look-a-likes for healthy relationships. When we look to people to fulfill our relational needs and to affirm us the way only God can, we make sad idols out of people … and they will, 100% of the time, let us down. People aren't meant to complete us or give us our identity ... we're supposed to walk out of the house with all that! If we don't, we will find ourselves in a problematic situation.

It's like going grocery shopping when you're hungry; it's always a bad idea. But, if you go to the store with your stomach full of a delicious home-cooked, fall-off-the-bone steak, you're not going to be so prone to grab the junk food. You know what a truly good and filling meal looks like, so you're not looking for a cheap imitation. Christ is the meal we continually dine on, so, when we leave the house, we're not tempted to settle for a cup-o-noodles. Not only that, but His love and how it meets us in our weakness teaches us the purity of real relationship.

When I'm vulnerable with the Lord and confess my dark thoughts, voice something I'm especially contending with, or just invite Him into a weak moment or season, He is faithful to meet me there and handle me with fine-tuned kindness. Because He meets me with gentleness and love, I am able to enter into more and more openness with Him; and, because He isn't cruel with me, I am never afraid to return to Him. This communion of my vulnerability met with His love is the center of who I am and how I function. I trust Him with all things, so I don't hide my vulnerability or sensitivity from those intimate friends the Lord entrusts me to love. Because I don't feel rejected by Him, I feel the freedom to be weak before Him ... knowing I am always accepted in Christ and have the freedom to live boldly and to walk at deep levels with people. God knows every square inch of my muck, and He still chooses me, so I live with zero to lose in any relationship with any person. I'm going to love boldly and live vulnerably because that's as close to the model of what Christ has shown me that I can live out. Walking with anyone, much less God, at an intimate, truly knowing-and-being-known level, I end up experiencing more of the Kingdom and of who God is than I thought possible. Because I feel protected and covered by God in my weakness, I want to cover others in their weakness. Because I have been met with kindness and Jesus' tender whisper to my heart, "I'm so sorry you're hurting right now," even when the hurt is my fault, I have the grace to empathize with those who are hurting. Because God has been a genuinely consistent friend in my life and through that consistency shown me His love, I know that consistency is a way to communicate love. Because I know that God isn't shocked, floored, disgusted, or turned away by my mess, I get to be listening ears and open arms to others. Because I have been forgiven and forgiven and forgiven, I get the joy of forgiving and forgiving and forgiving others. I am rightly loved for the purpose of rightly loving others. And I pursue Christ in intimacy to receive perfect relationship from Him, firstly, because He's the best, and, secondly, so that I can give as much of Him away as possible to those who need Him. See, culture tells us, "Give to get." That's karma, right? Put good out in the world so we get good back. In the Kingdom of God, we get in order to give ... and give and give. Choosing to walk in intimacy with God is the foundation of walking intimately with people.

Lord, I am so grateful You desire relationship with us. You desire one-on-one, unique, beautiful, powerful, intimate friendship. You love us with purity unmatched. I'm quite tired of the lie that attacks that Truth. God, please uniquely reveal Your desire for relationship to each reader. I ask that You specifically and powerfully reveal Your heart to every single person who reads this chapter.

Father, please make us emulators of how You do relationship and the purity with which You love. There is nothing more powerful than pure love.

Please make us acutely aware that You are pure love's Source.

LIFE, LIBERTY, AND
THE PURSUIT OF PURPOSE

9

"**M**ost modern freedom is at root fear. It is not so much that we are too bold to endure rules; it is rather that we are too timid to endure responsibilities." – G.K. Chesterton, *What's Wrong with the World*

I recall having an abstract view of freedom from the time I can remember. Growing up in the Church, I wasn't short on songs or messages that addressed the idea, but connecting freedom to a real and tangible application in my life seemed almost impossible. In my mind, freedom was something we sang about, claimed, and declared, but outside of it empowering people to dance through the aisles with banners of "Jehovah-Jireh," freedom seemed largely absent in the Church. I had heard and believed, to an extent, that, once we received salvation, we were supposed to also receive freedom from the powers of sin that weighed us down. In my mind, this would translate into me not getting so easily upset, not struggling with the same sexual temptations that had become all too familiar, and being able to finally control my words and actions. In general, I thought freedom meant I'd become a more pleasant, cheerful person. I heard so many sermons about how Jesus died to set us free, but I didn't see many people walk in that freedom, or at least freedom as I thought it should be.

The expectation I had was a life free from struggle as opposed to walking in freedom, though I'd still struggle. I heard that we didn't have to be held captive by our sin nature and habitual struggles. I was told that we could have peace in and out of every season regardless of circumstance, but I didn't fully see that peace in reality. I now realize that what I had believed to be freedom was actually perfection. I was looking at the fruit of brokenness and human fallibility instead of the fruit of a redemptive Father who steadily, and in His timing, makes all things work together for the good of those He loves and are called according to His purpose.[65] Due to my being critical, I was just endlessly disappointed by people and myself.

I truly believed that, and I know that I'm not alone in this, once I fully gave my life over to Jesus, I would have no more problems with the same old sins that I had fought with for so long. As I'm sure you know, once you've grappled a long time with something that has proven to be a harmful thing in your life, you look for hope that you don't have to struggle forever. *There's someone who has paid the price for me to live free and clear? I'll take some of that!* That was truly how I felt. I wanted a body transplant. I wanted for all the years of habitual sin and wrong thinking to be gone in an instant. But I had freedom wrong. Although salvation happens in an instant, our living a free lifestyle on a consistent basis takes a rerouting of old behaviors and changing of unhealthy patterns into new and healthy habits. Freedom in Christ entails a re-ordering of life from the inside out. When we surrender to Christ, we are given an all-access pass to freedom. We are given full authority to have it, claim it, walk in it, and stay in it. Go with me on this, but I think we treat freedom as though it's a rollercoaster track we're made to just snap onto for the ride. I know I have. Whereas, freedom is like a road on which we drive. We can stay on the road and go where it leads, but, when we get distracted and veer off onto another path, we don't then look back at the road and blame it for not doing what it was supposed to do. Or even worse, we don't blame Jesus for the decisions we made or for the consequences of those decisions in not partnering with Him ... or, do we? Our freedom is a partnership with Jesus via the Holy Spirit, and it's one we're meant to steward. (BTW: You're welcome for the rollercoaster analogy ... my 12-year-old self is so proud of me.)

I'm only as free as I am surrendered to Christ.

There's that good ole' word *surrender* again. Now hear me on this, and know I am not meaning to condescend. If you've made it this far in the book, I am sure you have a fairly solid understanding of the work of Jesus Christ on the cross. When Adam and Eve sinned, freedom was lost. Sin shattered all possibility of freedom because sin separated them (and us) from freedom's source: God. No one could be truly free until Jesus died and rose again.

Since Jesus is the One who secured our ability to taste that freedom again, via His own death and resurrection, that makes Him the sole proprietor of freedom; and, although He gives it freely, freedom belongs to and was won by Him alone. So why then, if I first receive freedom through Christ, would I expect to have it outside of Him and His will for my life? We can't expect to entertain what we know isn't healthy for us, do what we want when we want to, and simultaneously be happy and joyful. That's just not how it works in the Kingdom. If we want the joy that comes as a by-product of relationship with the Lord, we must be IN relationship with the Lord. Surrendering to Jesus entails more than salvation from hell. It's a surrender to a completely new life empowered by the Spirit. To surrender to Jesus means He's not just my Savior. Jesus is also my Lord. On a practical level, that's walking in a daily friendship that means actually spending time with the Lord, talking and listening to Him, allowing His thoughts to shape yours, living based off what HE says is best for your life and not what you think is best for your life, surrendering unhealthy thoughts as quickly as you can, choosing to look to Him and His will in all you do. The more opportunity you give yourself to be in intentional communion with God, the more your heart will begin to align with His. The focus of your life will shift from searching for freedom to enjoying and safeguarding your freedom by simple relationship with the One who gave freedom to you.

I have had many times I've gotten to what I considered to be a comfortable place with the Lord, times when I start to feel somewhat good about how I'm living and confident in my ability to stay on the "straight and narrow" with my thought life and actions. Just so you know, if you want to discern when the devil is about to try and trip you, look for these moments in your life. Comfort brings complacency, and complacency is the welcome mat for demonic attack. The second I disconnect from communion with the Lord is the moment I start seeing my relationship with Him as a compliment to my life and not life itself.

Once I've reduced God to a secondary source of life to reference only when needed as opposed to the primary source of life, I immediately, and without fail, start to deteriorate at a rapid speed.

Once we taste true intimacy with the Lord and the freedom that is in Him, and we walk away, whether intentionally or passively, the lack felt is unbearable. It's no different than if you were someone raised in a room without windows. You'd intellectually know about the concept of sunlight, but you'd never see it. You would be accustomed to and contented with the limitations of walls, the inability to truly stretch your legs, or to never feel the sun on your face. But if you're taken outside for even a moment and see the beautiful landscape surrounding your windowless room, your perspective would irreversibly shift. You'd no longer be content in the small world you had known for so long. If you're then told to go back inside that closed-off and windowless world to live out your existence, it will be a soul-crushing blow. Now you've seen there is more. No one can tell you that the world you've known is the only world there is. You may be overwhelmed by all the things you don't know about the outside world and the rules that come with all the new territory you're exposed to, but that doesn't discourage you. If the creator of this place welcomes you to know how he designed this world to flourish and warns you against what will hinder or harm its flourishing, you won't roll your eyes and claim his design is bondage. You'd welcome all guidelines because you desire to enjoy and participate in this new world in the best way possible, to its fullest. Our moving from a dead life of sin to a free life in Christ is no different.

Yet so many of us, having never been fully free and living within the confines of our own sin patterns and shortcomings for so long, taste our first bit of freedom and want free reign to control it. We don't want to be told how to steward our freedom and what we must do to guard our freedom. We especially don't want to be told that our being free has anything to do with what we actually do. We, like petulant children, want life our way. We want to live within the familiar boundaries we set. We prefer our own definitions of what is "safe." We don't want to give up our comfortable relationship with sin. In fact, we do away with the "s" word all together and call sin a "mistake," "quirk," or our "personality." In other words, we want to be able to roam in and out of God's definition of freedom at our leisure. Without our fully knowing it, because that's how the devil does his best work, we slowly move back into our windowless world, and one day look up to realize we can't see the mountains anymore. The sunlight is gone, and all because we wanted God's freedom and our way at the same time.

Partnering with the Lord in our freedom is something that is integral to our walk with Him. If we want the benefits of the Kingdom while on earth, that means we have to operate with Kingdom principles. We're not yet in heaven, where the struggle to choose good and reject evil won't be a struggle anymore. Heaven: where we won't hurt and we won't hurt anyone else; where our shame will be gone, and the work Jesus finished on the cross will be fully realized in us; where we'll be holy, like our Father, and move and think in His holiness; everything we do and say will flow out of perfect joy in God's perfection. In heaven, we won't have to choose to prefer God. He will be our Perfect Preference, our First Love.

The gift and grace of God is such that, once we receive Christ in our lives, we have the authority to walk in Kingdom reality now, but it takes effort on our part. Not that we have to strive to stay inside the lines because, believe it or not, there is much more freedom within the boundaries God has set up than there is outside those boundaries.

Think about someone operating in a major addiction. Let's be real here, we're all close to addiction if we're not willing to lay our will down. But the point is, the world would celebrate your freedom and ability to do what you want with your body, eat what you want, drink what you want and as much as you want, and they would call that freedom. However, if you were to speak with an addict, they would tell you a different story. Addicts contend daily for their lives and wrestle with the inner voices that say, *A drink or 10 will make this better. This one pill will make me feel okay for a bit. This binge-meal is just what I need to take the edge off. That affair will validate me in a way my wife can't. Don't worry! Porn is victimless.* Addicts will tell you firsthand they aren't free. In fact, addicts are held captive by the very things they once called freedoms.

I think we'd all be surprised by the amount of people who walk around upset with the Lord for how miserable they are in life; meanwhile, they're doing things they know aren't healthy, holding onto mindsets Jesus asked them to lay down, and being disobedient whether in their hearts, actions, or both. Once I fully gave Jesus my life, my will had to bow down to His at every crossroad. When it doesn't, I see and feel the ramifications of my unsubmitted will in my own life. If my expectations inform my view of God's goodness, I have made idols out of my expectations.

This idolatry of expectations works because of a distorted view of two facts about God: 1) God is good; and 2) God does what is good. Idolatry happens when I assume that what I think is good for me is also what God thinks is good for me. In other words, God is good to me as long as He and I both agree on what is best for me. So, if I don't get into the college I want, get the job I think I'm perfect for, or marry the spouse who I believe to be the right one for me, and I'm disappointed with God or myself or others, then I have made an idol out of those expectations. I might claim to worship God, but my idolatry causes my definition of "what's good" to be the functional god in my life. This is a problem. But expectations turned idols don't just start with something that we think could be a healthy expectation. An idol can easily be formed when we start to expect something bad for ourselves. This looks more like, *Well of course I'm not going to get into the school I want to attend; of course, I'm not going to get the job I want or the spouse I'm actually supposed to have.* We can easily be more concerned about holding onto an "inevitable" failure because we're afraid of disappointment. If we only expect to fail, we'll never have to face disappointed hopes.

I'd like to take this moment to address an argument that I feel rising even as I write this sentence. You could look me in the face and boldly say, "Well, maybe YOU need help to do and live rightly, but I've got a good grip on my life. I'm happy for the most part, don't walk with any vices, am fairly successful on my own, and have pretty good control over the decisions I make." To that I say, well done. I respect your self-control. However, I would argue that freedom for you might look a bit more external than internal, but the need for freedom in both our lives is the same. It's easy to address outward issues and things we can see and tangibly address, but what about the heart? In my experience, those who have a great deal of control in their lives tend to like having control in about every area of their lives. Those people who have it "together" outwardly are sometimes the ones who are emotionally holding on by a thread. So maybe you don't need freedom in an area that I've mentioned. But maybe you need freedom from control or from the need to be as close to perfect as possible. Maybe you need freedom from emotional manipulation. Maybe you need freedom in your ability to receive love. Maybe you need freedom from habitually lying. Maybe you need freedom from superiority and the isolation it brings. Maybe you need freedom from needing acceptance by everyone you meet. Maybe you need freedom from selfishness. I could continue for a quite a while, but the point is, wherever you are and whatever bondage you're struggling to free yourself from ...

Christ has already paid for your freedom.

Now, having believed that Christ has guaranteed our freedom, the job of taking hold of that freedom is now in our hands. We started the chapter talking about how our perception of freedom can look quite informative compared to the actual freedom we experience. Poor thought patterns and faith that's limited by fear end up inhibiting our growth. Not believing rightly about God and His character is like a gnarly weed left untended. It may be a small eye sore at first, something that you'd like to divert attention from, but it will go from an inconvenience to a crippling disease that spreads and prohibits new growth. It will end up crowding, overtaking, and infecting all parts of you unless it's *fully* uprooted. The "fully" part of that mandate is where we get so hung up. We may pull a weed or two and then look up and see how much more uprooting has to be done. Then we become discouraged. But this is where in our walk with the Lord, if we persist and chase after our freedom in Christ, we will not only see that freedom, but we'll also see God with a wider and taller lens. Why would we not want to see a clearer, fuller, and more 3-dimensional image of who God is? That's when you'll have those worship moments that feel as though you're in a completely different atmosphere. That's when you'll have moments of breakthrough and feel a burst of amazing endorphins and encouragement. But, if you leave those moments there and not stewarded, they will only ever be moments, not a lifestyle. We're called to a lifestyle of freedom and not a life spent chasing the moments that we felt the freest, or the ones that we think are going to be THE experience with God that is going to finally set us free.

Now Millennials, this is an area we need to discuss briefly. For some reason, the majority of us live with a great deal of, *Well, I'll wait to deal with this thing tomorrow, the next day, week, or maybe year?* We can be a procrastinating generation, bullied into stagnancy by fear. So, we've been afraid to fail, and we've grown up with incredibly fragile shells that have been built by culture's unconscious decision to uncover us in our growing, struggling, and failing. The defense mechanisms we've built up in order to steer us away from being hurt or let down not only limit us, but they teach us to expect less freedom, less joy, less hope for ourselves. Many people in the Church have not given us room to fail. We have youth groups with teenagers leading worship and learning how to stand on their own faith. We expect the same fruit and consistency from them as we do from a man or woman who has walked with the Lord for decades. We tend to demonize and punish those who are struggling with their faith. We tend to turn our noses up at those who still say the occasional curse word, struggle in a way we don't understand, or haven't progressed past whatever spiritual milestone WE deem appropriate. We've got to be done with that arrogance. Now, I'm not saying to blindly entrust leadership and promotion to any and every person. But I am saying that maybe, if we prayed more and asked God to point out purpose and calling in our up-and-coming leaders, as opposed to focusing on the parts still under renovation, we would save a lot of people some hurt and difficulty in knowing God for who He truly is. When we lead from arrogance, we end up forcing ourselves and the ones we're bringing up in the Church to contend with a lot more frustration than need be. Think about it. You may be a worship pastor and have some talented people getting involved, but you promote someone too early and end up walking through a much more painful experience on the other side. In a lot of cases, the one being punished or sat down for a season ends up walking away from the Church and sometimes God altogether. Of course, we need to, at the right moment, confront sin and call it for what it is. But the motive in confronting sin is to help the struggling person run into God's open, forgiving arms for grace. We confront sin because sin hurts people. We don't confront sin to hurt people. It is the Church's responsibility to make it easy and inviting for people to follow Jesus. When anyone, myself included, creates a roadblock for another person getting to know Jesus, I have a problem with that.

If we're supposed to encounter people and engage with them in the love Christ died to communicate, that means we must emulate Jesus in all we do. I have a difficult time with anyone who doesn't make forgiveness and restoration easily accessible and possible. Now notice, I did not say easily accomplished. I said, easily accessible. The doorway to redemption, forgiveness, and freedom can always be found in Jesus through repentance. However, to experience and taste what God has for us on the other side of forgiveness, we must walk through and not stop at the door of forgiveness. When we stop shy of what God has in store for us, God doesn't shrink back or suddenly become not good. He doesn't change His mind about the level of freedom we deserve to experience; that's on us. If we're not walking as freely as we know we should be, it's not because God doesn't want to lead us to deeper and greater levels of consistent freedom. So, don't worry. Whether you're a pastor who has led poorly or one of the poorly led, it's okay. We're all moving toward the same finish line, but the Lord brings us across that finish line in different ways. So be careful when you think someone is progressing more slowly than they ought to progress. I just wonder what would happen if we stopped putting down others in their process of growing, changing, failing, and learning and started partnering with them in the process with love and truth? Everyone should be given the opportunity to meet Jesus and His redemption through the kindness and love of His people. We are never given a license, no matter how justified it may feel, to withhold from others the patience, longsuffering, forgiveness, redemption, restoration, and safety to heal and grow that we have been so freely given in Christ. If your own "mastering" of your life entitles you to portion out your forgiveness and grace to others based on how you feel, you're not being obedient to the right voice. Maybe, if we spent more time being sure we've heard the Lord on behalf of those we're leading, we wouldn't spend so much time defending our leadership to those who are hurt in the wake of our recklessness.

Now, I realize I went on a bit of a tangent there, but it comes from the reality that we are meant to participate with Christ in our freedom. We learn at different paces. We find and exercise freedom at different times. That's why Paul is so clear in his urging to us to "work out our own" salvation."[66] If I try to work out YOUR salvation, I will be trying to fix a "you" issue from a "me" perspective. Yes, it's incredibly valuable to have accountability with others who have a rock-solid foundation in the Word. Yes, we can do right simply because we're told what is right, we believe we're being given accurate information, and trust the person giving us that advice. That wisdom saves us a lot of heartache on our road to getting where God wants to take us. But doing something because we're told it is right and out of fear of punishment makes us merely rule followers. That kind of living doesn't distinguish us from exceptional and competent middle school students. However, when we make a healthy choice, refrain from something we know is harmful, or follow a biblical principle because we trust the Source, the Holy Spirit, we become worshippers. I'm not trying to be a rule follower. I'm trying to be a worshipper. I want everything I do and say to be checked, corrected, adjusted, informed, and encouraged by the Holy Spirit. If we arrogantly impose our upbringings, biases, and preferences on others and call these things "freedom," we might as well take our entire wardrobe of shirts and shoes and run around forcing people to try on our clothes. We'll be upset when our stuff doesn't fit properly on them. I'm not done with my clothing analogy, so buckle up.

When you first accept Christ as your Savior, it's like you're instantly taken into the largest room you've ever seen and given countless yards of a beautiful fabric designed especially for you. It has an intricate pattern, and it fits your body perfectly, covering all your insecure areas. The colors showcased within the print are a perfect match to pull out every nuanced hue in your eyes. You are given that fabric without question because it was made for you. That's your identity. You are given every tool in the Word of God to stitch your garment without harming the fabric. You're given the pattern and creativity from the Holy Spirit. Jesus is with you as you cut and form the fabric. The Father is there ready to redeem your wrong cuts, ill-fitting designs, and all the scraps you discard.

God, the Creator, speaks creatively, and He knows how to communicate to His children in a language they understand.[67] I know that if God can arrest my heart by speaking my language, I'm not the only one He wants to arrest.

God, I thank You for freedom.

Thank You. Thank You. Thank You for freedom.
Thank You for winning it for us, giving it freely,
showing us how to steward it, and being patient
and gracious when we steward freedom poorly.
Lord, please reveal areas for each of us where
we are settling for less freedom than You
have for us. Please turn on the lights and point
flashlights in the dormant corners of our lives
we've let go dark. You want us to live and walk
in full freedom, and that's where we're meant
to thrive. Lord, I ask for a freedom revolution
in each person reading this chapter, God,
and I thank You for it.

10

At this point, we have covered some intense things. We've delved into hard and uncomfortable conversations, some of which a few of us may have preferred not to have altogether; but this is the first part of a beautiful process. When we hear the truth, there's an initial switch that seems to make us aware of our own accountability to the truth. This accountability causes more curiosity and opens us to hear the Lord. Sometimes we become so shut down spiritually that it takes a lot of sitting with our thoughts until we ask Him to exchange them for His thoughts. It doesn't make sense to the world that one would have to tire themselves out before they'd finally choose God. As I've mentioned in previous chapters, there is a perceived weakness attached to someone realizing their own need for God. But I would like to argue that real strength is acknowledging your need for grace. Admitting this need and going to the Source of grace takes courage. Submitting your will to God is not a weak move; it's a strong one.

I also think it's important to say this: Jesus is practical. He didn't design us to be independent, living our lives far away from Him, on our own. We're not going to get to heaven and have a catch-up coffee with God about all He missed in our lives while we were off doing our own thing.

Whatever you may have experienced growing up, God is not an absentee dad. No, He is quite the opposite. See, God the Father is interested in daily friendship. He's interested in you letting Him be a part of, not only your Sunday morning, but your Friday night. He wants to be with you in your biggest life victories and the moments where you feel crushed under the weight of the world. He's looking to run this race with you.

Sometimes I get frustrated with my limited ability to accurately articulate how much I believe Jesus wants relationship with us. If you were to take all the ways Jesus feels about you and put those feelings out in front of yourself as a whirling 3-dimensional picture, you would begin to see the expanse and variety of ways in which Jesus loves you. Go with me on this, but I picture it almost like a variety of different colored, shaped, and sized dust or fog clouds spinning, all intertwined into each other. All the while, as they move in and out of each other, every cloud keeps its shape and identity. Picture it, and don't overthink what you see. One cloud may look powder blue and circular in shape. It moves throughout the rest of the airy bodies at a rapid pace, almost like a bouncing ball. Every time you see it, you simultaneously feel seen and chosen. One cloud may be a muted magenta color that looks like the most ornate orchid. It moves and passes in front of and behind other clouds. As you see it move, you feel safe at your core. You could see a metallic puzzle piece floating in front of you, shimmering and reflecting the colors of other passing clouds, fitting into the different formations being made by other clouds. Every time you see it, you immediately feel like your dad is proud of you.

Yes, I know the word picture here is asking for a lot of your imagination, but the point of describing it this way is to break down any remaining preconceived scaffolding in our perception of how Jesus expresses His love. His love for us is on a macro, yet equally micro level, specific and individual. God's love for you is better than your best dream of love or your deepest desire for intimacy. It may come in different colors, hues, shapes, and ways in our lives, and that's something we should see as a gift. If you could see God's love, you would be able to see the purity of motive and the genuinely good nature in every thought He has about you. You would see how He sees you and how His perspective of you shapes what He does for you and in your life. His love is tailored to an exact fit for each of us when we choose to know Him. He loves us each the way we need to be loved and in the way that connects with our individual hearts, the hearts He designed in the most honest and beautiful way to beat for Him.

I'm so grateful that God knows how to love me specifically and intentionally. He knows the times when I need to have a fire lit under me; and, other times, He cradles my heart with tenderness. He knows how to soothe my heart when I can't bear one more sarcastic comment about my identity. Oh yes, because let us not forget that those who can seemingly be the most vocal and unafraid of offending others are usually the ones more sensitive and easily offended. I know this fact because one temptation I struggle with is using sarcasm to cut others down. Since I know this issue personally, I find it quite a beautiful quality of the Lord that He chooses to walk in patience with me despite my glaring insufficiencies and hypocrisies. I can talk about everything I believe to be true about who God is, but I would be a fool to negate the other parts of my life that would fly in contradiction to what I believe. That's because, even though I know the Truth, I don't always do what I know to be true. What I do isn't always what I know I should do, and such is life.[68]

At this point, I've written some 200 pages of text and spent over a year putting onto paper what I believe God has downloaded to my heart. That doesn't mean I feel like I've conquered or become an expert in anything I've communicated. There's a lot that I've shared because I've watched, learned, or lived it firsthand. My story of who I know God to be and how I've seen Him move in my life are non-negotiable truths that cannot be separated from me ... which may explain my passionate tone. But I'm trying, and in this writing, attempting to taste real faith. I want that sort of faith that calls things as though they were even when they're not quite so yet.[69] This book, from start to finish, has been a practical faith exercise for me.

That's not exactly what you want to hear the author of an inspirational book say, is it? I know, because if I had read that from an author, I'd be like, "Wait, so you're still a hot mess, and you're trying to tell me something about Truth?" The reason I can be honest with you about my struggles and share the truth with conviction is because I'm writing my story covered by grace. I'm writing my story not because I've won every battle in my life, but because Jesus has won for me. Jesus always wins despite my successes or failures. He knows the type of encouragement I need and doesn't get put out with me even when His correction falls upon deaf ears. You know those miracles in the Bible about Jesus opening blind eyes and deaf ears? I know those miracles happened because they are still happening to me.

When your eyes open to God's love, you will see that Jesus' desire to be near you isn't based off anything other than His genuine love for you. You will see that He loves you with the same fervency of a true suitor while also not being angry with you when you back away from relationship. You'll see patience that isn't contrived by selfish motives. You'll see heartbreak and the deep levels of purity in pain He experiences when you walk in any bit of darkness. This response isn't rooted in God's disappointment, disapproval, or frustration, but rather His desire to see you live in the fullness He paid for you to experience.[70] In short, you will see how genuinely wonderful Jesus is and that everything He has done, asked, and said in His Word is for your good and His Father's glory.

In the first chapter, I told you that I would be honest with you throughout our journey together. As we near the end, you might be wondering something like, *Okay, well what's all of this for? What's he trying to get me to do? What's the 'ask'?* I understand that we've traversed the ground of quite a few difficult topics. I'm sure, at times I've pressed some buttons or maybe made you feel just plain uncomfortable. I know that the way I communicate can sometimes come across as structured chaos. I started this book knowing only that I was supposed to tell my story, and that my story isn't linear. It's not something that has progressed in a conventional, outlined, almost predictable path. My hope has been that this writing would bring some of my struggles to the forefront in the hopes that even one person feels less alone. My prayer is that God would take the vulnerability I've chosen to walk in and the gut wrenching parts of my life as a testimony of His goodness to call hearts back to Him. So yes, I know this book is equal parts testimony, painful truth, unconventional thinking, practical theology, and an encouragement to pursue the "more" of Christ at all costs[71] ... but it's really meant to serve as Holy Spirit-inspired lighter fluid to ignite a fire in your heart. I want you to come to Life.

God has been more constant than any person in my life has ever been or ever could be. He is the constant Encourager, reminding me that I am called to be loved and to love in return.[72] His kindness leads me to repentance, and it's His kindness that daily sustains me.[73] He has never left me alone in the dark.[74] He has held me when I've needed to be calmed and shown peace.[75] He keeps me grounded in Him while simultaneously teaching me how to fly.[76] He's the ultimate Friend and the Rock on whom I choose to build my life.[77]

You may be reading this chapter and find yourself in one of two camps. The first camp is someone who, in reading my story, has become acutely aware of their need and desire for a relationship with this amazing God. It doesn't mean you have communicated that desire to anyone or even realized it until this moment, but your heart's been stirred. If that's you, you may even feel your heart racing a bit right now and a gnawing feeling in your gut, so much so that you may be tempted to put this book down and walk away. But please don't walk away. This is your moment. This is your opportunity to enter the greatest relationship of your life. It's not the easiest relationship, mind you, but the most rewarding and fulfilling. No more preamble, now is your moment. If you're tired of the way things have been going in your life, and you know that you need someone bigger than yourself; if you are willing to give your heart to someone who can be trusted, let's do this. See, salvation isn't some mystical, creepy experience. The decision to surrender to Christ is beautiful, simple, and yields more life than any other decision one could make. So, I've written a prayer that would be like how I would talk to Jesus and invite Him into my life. You can repeat this prayer word-for-word or pray it in your own words. Just know that a prayer of salvation is about surrender and giving over control of your life while inviting Jesus to reside in your heart. It's a prayer of confession that Jesus is the Son of God and that He was crucified on the cross and rose again to redeem you. Jesus says in the book of Matthew that if we acknowledge or confess Him to others, He will be faithful to do so before the Father.[78] So pray and choose to believe the Gospel in your heart. Then tell someone ... believe you me, you'll want to tell someone. I couldn't shut up about Jesus when I met Him, and I still can't shut up about Him.

To be clear, the Gospel is the truth that God the Father sent His Son, Jesus, to live the only perfect human life that has ever been lived.[79] Though He never sinned, Jesus suffered and died to take the full penalty for all the sin that breaks this world and our own hearts. He rose from the dead, signaling that God's wrath against your sin and mine is completely removed forever.[80] You are not defined by the worst things you've done or the worst things that have been done to you. You're defined by Christ's perfect life. He takes your death and sin; you get His life and purity. Receiving Jesus as your Savior means you will now be in Christ.[81] When a person is in Christ, they are covered in the holiness that God the Father sees in the life of His Son.[82] Okay, now that you know what the "Gospel" means, here's the prayer:

Jesus, I don't understand everything, and I may not fully understand You yet, but I want to. I know in my heart that You are the Son of God and that You died for my sake, so we could not only do this life together, but for eternity. I ask that You forgive me. Please forgive me for the ways in which I've created a divide between us by my sin. I know I need You in my heart, and, not only that, I want You in my heart. I surrender and give You full access to me, to my brokenness, to my identity, to every part of who I am. You have all authority, and, in Your kindness, You have desired relationship with me. Now I choose You back. You're it for me, and I love you. Now I invite Your Holy Spirit to indwell me and my life and to teach me how to hear and obey Your voice. Thank You, Lord. Thank You for loving me first. Thank You for being God and for creating me with a purpose, a calling, and a perfectly crafted identity made to worship You. In Jesus' name, Amen.

Now to address the person in the second camp, this is a person who has grown up with the knowledge of Jesus. This person may even have said a version of the prayer I just mentioned, possibly multiple times. This person may have believed for a great deal of time that they are "good" with Jesus. There may not have been any spiritual fruit apparent in changed attitudes, actions, priorities, affections, dreams, but the person has prayed a prayer and believes they're in relationship with God. This was the camp I belonged to until I was 18. I prayed a prayer of salvation when I was four on my parent's bedroom floor that I remember to this day. But I hadn't fully surrendered my life to God. I know there are many young children who invite Jesus into their hearts and mean business with the Lord, but I was not one of them. The great danger of growing up in church and around a lot of people who live and operate with real, tangible faith is that it's easy to believe your proximity to faith means the assurance of your own. And because I love you, as I hope is evidenced in this writing, I cannot allow you to believe that lie any further. Just because your parents raised you in a Christian home doesn't make you a Christ-follower. Just because you're in church every weekend and cry when your favorite worship song gets to the bridge doesn't mean you're walking hand-in-hand with Jesus. And just because you acknowledge that there is some Higher Power doesn't mean you're connected to that higher power. You can't have a relationship with the ambiguity of a higher power. You can't receive life from a higher power, and you can't be saved by a nameless higher power. Higher Power has a name, and it is *Jesus*. He is the Highest Power, unmatched in authority. That's the bottom line, the Truth from which all truth is sourced. Without Him there is no truth, and, outside of Him, there is no assurance on this earth. If, like me, you thought you knew Jesus, and, in reading this book, you realize that you don't have a relationship with Him, the prayer you just read is for you, too.

The prayer isn't a magic incantation. It doesn't save a person. Jesus saves, and it's a person's surrender of their heart to Him which changes that person's whole life. The prayer is meant to help bring you into alignment with God and His intent for you to be fully surrendered to His sovereignty and goodness at all points. When we're submitted and in the right relationship as God's son or daughter, then we're exactly in the middle of divine purpose.

Relationship with Christ is what I want for you. That's the heart behind this whole book and why I've spent two years of my life pining over words and trying to steward what I believe God asked me to do. You and I both need a heart adjustment. By heart adjustment, I want God to do for our hearts what chiropractors do when they adjust spines. The process may look and feel uncomfortable. There may be cracks and popping of spiritual joints and ligaments. God's adjustments might initially feel more painful than helpful. But I think we all need an adjustment from time to time to rightly align our hearts with the One our hearts were created to worship. We're meant to challenge each other, to lift one another up. We're meant to believe the best in each other, to empathize with pain and heartache, to show up by way of honesty and not just comfortable, apathetic speech that sounds good. After all, I can ask you how you are when I see you on the street, but I might communicate the complete opposite with my body language and tone. Why do you think 99% of people respond to a question about how they're doing with, "I'm good" without ever asking themselves if they actually are? The reason most people don't honestly answer this question when asked is because they don't trust that the person who is asking genuinely cares about them. If we thought others had the time, cared to know, or were invested in how we were doing, it would radically change the way we live.

To be blunt, I've written this book to invest in your life. I consider the time I've spent writing this book as an investment in your growth and your heart condition. I don't know that everything I've said will be received with open arms and with the loving intention with which I wrote it. In fact, I know there are going to be things that you may take issue with, but that's okay. I've risked a lot to share the vulnerability of my story, one that I've tried for years to shield from the eyes and accusations of so many. But I will no longer submit to a culture that would tell me my experiences with God are invalid. I will not yield to the ever-changing wind of public opinion and what is currently accepted or championed. My walk with the Lord has been carved out in the context of my own life, the experiences I've had, the time I've spent in His Word, and my desire to know more than my own weakness.

But that's the beauty of faith, right? Although the sacrifice is made once and for all, the relationship is made individually and uniquely between the Lord and the person engaging in relationship with Him. Out of my hunger and desperation, I have found Living Hope to cling to. Out of my failings and struggles, I have chosen *to surrender* instead of fleeing. I have chosen to stay rooted in the Truth while I try to understand other facets of who God is. It has been a wild ride; and, if I know anything about the Lord, it will continue to be so. The only question now is what will you do with my story? How will you respond?

I was only able to cover a portion of the Truth there is for us to know. In fact, even calling it a portion is generous. There is so much to explore about God. There is so much He wants to reveal to you about your life. There is so much freedom, restoration, and new life He's wanting to give you. Surrender is not comfortable, but it's so rewarding. I pray you see that reality in my sharing because, I assure you, surrender can be disorienting, daunting, and downright terrifying at times. Still, true adventure, intimate relationship, and a life worth living are worth the surrender to have Jesus. I promise, Jesus is better than anything you will ever give up. Jesus is better. Jesus is best.

Lord, as we end this journey, I ask You to partner with the reader as they continue their journey with You. I ask for those who still havent chosen You...

that You would put exactly the right people in their lines to woo them to You.

I also ask that any unhealthy or detrimental voices against the readers growth be silenced. God, please pursue the hearts of those who have engaged with this book with a fervency that demands a response. I know You love us, and, beyond anything else I've asked throughout this book, I simply ask that Jesus' name and His goodness be on our lips from now into eternity.

I sure love You, Lord.

ACKNOWLEDGEMENTS

Now I'm a big fan of honoring others so, if you'll allow me, I'd like to do that right now. I've arrived at this point surrounded by a tribe that I love very much, and I'd like for you to know why:

Abby, thank you for being real and just such a steady and solid friend. You've shown me in beautiful ways how authenticity with the Lord and others is crucial.

Adri, you are one of the most selfless people I know, and you always leave me better than you found me. You inspire me to love beyond myself.

Akari, there's no one I've yet to meet as a friend who is as intentional and honoring with everyone they encounter. But it's who you are. I'm marked by your influence in my life.

Ali, you are such a light, and you have been in my life ever since I met you. Getting to know the purity of your heart and your desire for the "more" of the Lord challenges me to never settle.

Austin, you tapped me on the shoulder one night during worship out of obedience to the Lord to say, "You feel like God has asked you to do something, and you're not sure if it's Him or not. It's Him, and He's going to honor the fact that you've chosen to set yourself apart. He wants to thank you for your obedience." That night I sat down to start writing the first chapter. Thank you for your real friendship.

Blair, I love you, friend. Thank you for the real talks, encouragement, and for championing me at every level. So glad I know you.

Brian, thank you for the conversation that sealed my belief in what God had called me to say. While sitting around a dinner table, you gave me the bravery and affirmation to know I had heard the Lord. Thank you.

Colette, thank you for being such a ride-or-die friend. You have protected me, cared for me, loved me, listened to my rants, heard my heart, championed my calling, and never left my side for almost a decade. Grateful doesn't cut it ...

Croce Family, thank you for making me feel a part of your family from the moment I met you. Your love is forever imprinted on my heart.

Dad, what can an incredibly grateful son say to honor such an amazing father? "Thank you" will never cover how you've supported, championed, loved, protected, defended, stood by, and pushed me into knowing Whose I really am. You have provided the safest place for me to contend with the Lord and to really hear His voice for my life. You have always seen more potential in me than I've seen in myself, and you consistently honor and love me, even when I fully don't deserve it. You have sadly been my punching bag at times, but you've taken the punches just like the Lord has in times of frustration in my life. You have been steady, unmoved, and full of love. I love you and can't believe I get to have you as my Dad. Out of all the things I'm proud of, I'm proudest of being your son.

Uncle Dudley and Betsy Hall, you both have loved me as long as I can remember. You saw me when I didn't feel seen and gave me nothing but unconditional love. I know what it is to be Christ-like by watching your walk.

Frank J, you are forever my little bro and someone whom I love fiercely. I'm proud of the man you're becoming, and I'm grateful to get to see you grow up firsthand. Thank you for loving me well and for all the years you've made me smile, laugh, and roll my eyes. I wouldn't change any of it!

Grandpa, thank you for showing me the value of a tender heart and for not ever being afraid to show and communicate what God's doing in you through your vulnerability and sensitivity to the Holy Spirit. The heritage of faith in our family is owed to you.

Grandma, thank you for loving me and for being such a great source of unconditional love. I miss your laugh, your cooking, but most of all the joy you used to exude. We're going to have some great times in heaven. I can't wait to hear your laugh again.

The Inprov team, Leigh, Jessica, Brandon, Tyler, and Kristi, thank you for your skill, creativity, and effort to help make this book a reality. I'm grateful for your covering in this process.

Jason and Victoria, thank you for showing me how to live boldly in the truth of who Christ is regardless of environment. You both have taught me how to explore the wonders of who God is and to love people fiercely, exactly where they are. The world is better and Christ is honored because you're who you are.

Janice, you have one of the purest hearts of anyone I know, and you have served as a source of joy in our family from as early as I can remember. Thank you for not being too adult to play with me, to hear what I had to say, to joke around with me, to spend time pouring into me. I haven't forgotten and never will. Love you.

Jenn, the night we met, you told me we were going to be friends. You chose me, and, as someone who hasn't felt overly "chosen," you spoke new identity on me that night. You also told me that night that I was Peter Pan and not a lost boy. You told me that I knew I was Peter Pan and that I needed to stop living like a lost boy. You snapped my focus into place. Thank you for being the one who told me I was meant to fly.

Joe, you're someone who I always feel instantly at peace with when I'm around you. Thank you for being the most inclusive person I know and for showing me that kindness doesn't cost anything. I've learned a lot about making people feel valued from you.

Joe and Pat, my Jersey family, I'll never forget a rough night while I was living in New York. Within an hour, you both had driven into the city to pick me up and take me to the beach. You didn't even ask me. You just came because you knew I needed it. That's who you are. You are true family, and I love y'all.

JoNell and Rick, you have been such a steady source of support and love for me. You have shown up when it wasn't convenient. You have fought to know me and my heart. You have played the role of interpreter on my behalf to my parents, and you always allowed me a safe place to land. Thank you. Thank you. Thank you. I love you both so very much.

Jonathan, thank you for your leadership as a brother. You have fought to truly know the Lord since I can remember, and you have always challenged me to do the same. Thank you for your vulnerability and for your honesty with me. I love you.

Josh, you are simply just someone I love very much. Thank you for the long talks, for the conversations that have challenged me, for believing in me, and for never letting me settle for less than every bit of who God has called me to be.

Kayla, thank you for being fiercely protective of me, for believing in what God has put on my life, and for teaching me that authenticity is never worth the trade-in of looking like you have it together. Whether you know it or not, you have taught me how to be real, even when it hurts.

Kari, I love you with my whole heart. Although I've known you since birth, the way you loved me coming out of high school and in the midst of a lot of darkness will never be forgotten. You were a safe haven and respite for me. You gave me a place and showed me my value. God only knows what you did for my heart.

Kelly, you are seriously just one of my favorite people to talk with about anything. We could (and have) spent literal days on end talking about everything under the sun. I feel so safe with and cared for by you. There is no one else in this world I would rather watch trashy television with while catching up on every bit of life. You're a gift, plain and simple.

Kevin and Dani, I love you and your family so much. Thank you both for loving on me throughout the years and for always making me feel at home with you. I'm grateful for y'all.

Laura, thank you for being love encapsulated. You make me feel seen, you're not scared of uncomfortable conversations, and you have been such a fun surprise big sister in my life. I love watching you shine, but, more than that, I love watching you love. You do it well.

LD, thank you for being a fast friend who chose me to love and who does so effortlessly. I am constantly impressed and challenged by how thoughtful you are, how intentional you are, and how faithful you are to serve and be exactly who God has created you to be. You're also the only person who can really get away with calling me "bud." Don't tell the others.

Leigh, thank you for believing in me from day one, for choosing to love me, and for doing so ferociously. Thank you for saying, "yes" to being my editor. You have been by my side, my right and left arm. You're my sounding board, my incredibly safe place, the person I call when I need to go to the depths of what I'm feeling and understand it. You're an image-bearer of Christ and have championed me across this finish line. This book is as much yours as it is mine because your fingerprints are throughout. Your fingerprints are on my heart, the very one I've poured out on these pages. Thank you.

Little Ones, you have already taught me so much about the goodness of God in your short lives so far. I learn from each of you and love you dearly. Thank you for letting me be your Uncle Cannonball.

Mallory, thank you for the great talks and for being an awesome sister-in-law. You've truly enriched our family by being in it. I'm glad to have a big sister in you!

Mama J and Senior, I just want to thank you both for welcoming me into your family from day one. Thank you for giving me the safest of places to just be, to feel seen, to feel understood. You have loved me well, and I'm forever marked by your friendship.

Pastor Mark and Jodie, thank you for loving me and for showing what it truly means to be submitted to God in all things. Thank you, Pastor Mark, for choosing to know me the first day you met me, for choosing to see value in me, and for giving me a seat at the table. Not only that, thank you for speaking purpose on me and for seeing this whole ministry thing long before many others did. Ms. Jodie, thank you for being a no-nonsense, real, but wholly loving momma bear in my life. I love you both.

Melissa, you're a breath of fresh air in my life. Thank you for being willing to cut up and for continually being so loving towards me. You've never made me feel like I'm anything other than loved by you.

Memaw and Papaw, thank you for being some of the best grandparents anyone could ask for. You have shown me unconditional love, you've taught me how to dominate in cards, you have laughed with me and taught me so much about the world, and you have been and always will be an inspiration of steadiness and faithfulness. I hope to carry your mantle and think it an honor.

Mom, I don't even know where to start. You have taught me how to be and how to love, simply. You have been patient and shown me grace when I haven't deserved it. You have been steady when I'm flailing. You have been my greatest defender and the one who taught me how to serve and love with a fire that points directly back to the Lord. The verse you live out to me and always have is John 3:30, "He must increase, but I must decrease." You have walked that truth out your whole life, and it's just one of the most beautiful things I've ever witnessed. You have served our family and everyone else in your life with selflessness at its purest form. You are the person I look at and think, Jesus must be really proud of that one. I know I am. I love you very much.

Natalie, you're one of my favorite people to cut up with and to have hard conversations with about life. Thank you for hearing my heart and for letting me hear yours. Thank you for never letting me off the hook and for the laughs I've needed in desperate times. Love you, friend.

Nathaniel, thank you for taking time with me growing up. Thank you for letting me tag along with you and for letting me hear your heart and know what you thought about life. Growing up, thank you for just always being someone I was glad to see and who I felt was glad to see me. There are few people on this earth who can hold a matchstick to your wit, and I'd like to think you passed a little of it off to me. For that and so much more, thank you.

Nick J, thank you for pushing me out of complacency. Thank you for seeing value in me when I couldn't see it in myself. Thank you for being a fierce voice of reason and for never letting me go too far into my head. Your levelness has been an anchor for me when I've needed it the most. Our friendship has been one of the great joys in my life because God's fingerprints have just always been on it. You never cease to be used by Him to encourage me, to make me feel seen and known when I've needed it, and to just overall challenge me. You're my brother, and I love you; that's it.

Nikki, God knew exactly what I needed when He sent us whirling into each other's lives, and I couldn't be more grateful. Thank you for being the first person to act-a-fool with me in public, for always being down to hear my heart, for bringing me into your family, for being a reprieve when I've so needed it, for constantly speaking value into me, and for seeing on me what I hadn't seen on myself. You've spoken a lot of life over me, lived a lot of life with me, and loved me through it all.

Rachel, you, my dear, are such a sweet gift to me. You were kind, welcoming, inclusive, and intentional with me from the second we met. Thank you for being a lifer, for being steady in my life, and for always being someone who I can laugh and be ridiculous with. I love you, lady!

Rita, I'm not quite sure I'll ever be able to thank you properly or to convey what you've done to my heart this side of heaven. You chose to love me a long time ago, and you have not let me go since. You have championed me, defended me, and stood up and said, "Absolutely not" when my character has been brought into question. You have given me words and challenges that have truly shaped who I've become. You've fought for me when I couldn't fight for myself, and you continue to do so. Thank you for letting me cry in your living room, call you anytime just to talk about whatever I'm facing, and for being a friend, an aunt, a mom, a grandmother, and an overall confidant. Thank you for honoring me from the start and for giving me a place at any table you're at. You are truly one of the realest representatives of Jesus I've encountered on this earth. I would go with you into any battle and back you in any cause. I honor you, Rita.

Pastor Robert, thank you for the years of investment your ministry has made in my life. You've helped ground me in the Truth with your gifting to communicate the Gospel and biblical theology. I'm inspired by your genuine love for Jesus and people. Thank you for being a spiritual father to me and the house of Gateway Church.

Ry, thank you for being obedient to the Lord all those years ago. Thank you for showing me what it looked like to love Jesus and be real in an uncompromising way. We have lived a whole lot of life with each other, and it doesn't matter how long it's been since we've talked, if I get to see you often or not, or what's going on in our lives... you are just my big brother, the one God used to walk me into the Kingdom. That's never changing. If there's anything good that comes from this book, you should know it's because of your initial investment into my life. God used you to heal so many parts of my heart and to show me how to love people fiercely and without agenda. Your heart is a rare and beautiful thing I'm so honored to know.

Ruben, you have been just such a gift in my life. You understand the way I think, what I hear in my head and how to talk me down. You give me room to just be with zero judgment. You are thoughtful and intentional with me in a way that is truly humbling. You have taught me I can't always be the strong one and to rely on those who love me to do just that. We've only known each other a few years, but, in that short time, God has used you to love on me in such a specific and personal way. You make me feel truly known, understood, and valued all at once. You're also my favorite person to make all the bad dad jokes with. You should be receiving your trophy in the mail soon.

Sam, you're my oldest friend, and you have literally seen me in every phase of my life. Even when we were little kids, you had the purest and most genuine of hearts. As we've grown, I've seen your heart shape and become more and more clear. You are just about one of the most kind and loving men I know. You never leave someone worse than you found them. You are about as selfless as they come, and you are the epitome of a low-maintenance, no pressure friend. You have never once condemned or put me down for anything I do. You have been a great sounding board in my life and you're one of my favorites to just hash it all out with. Thank you for loving me well for 29 years and counting.

Sarah, thank you for being exactly the roommate I needed for a season and for being a friend who knows me and all my quirks, makes fun of them all, but loves me still. You are by far my favorite rollercoaster riding partner and my favorite person to watch movies with. You quote lines with me without missing a beat, are always down to pause the movie to have a serious talk or just simply go over a prospective Ramen order. THESE ARE BIG THINGS FOR ME. I'll go to Bridges with you and cry outside the house from Mrs. Doubtfire any ole time. I can't wait to be old and crotchety with you, yelling at little teenagers who need to hear it. Just at the end of it all in our best Jimmy Dugan, "That's GOOD ADVICE!"

Stef, when I think about you, I think about the clear eyes with which Jesus sees us. Although you are incredibly justice-minded, you choose to see the best in every person and situation. You are slow to make a judgment, slow to speak, and quick to love. Thank you for giving me a home in yours and for being a big brother I know who completely has my back and who will always point me towards loving purely.

Tia, the night we met you said we were going to be good friends, and you meant it. I'm not sure either of us expected that some 11 years later we would still want to travel, laugh with, and live next to each other, but here we are! You are truly such an incredible friend to me. You have taught me how to grow up in so many major ways, and I'll never be able to thank you enough. Thank you for teaching me boundaries and their importance. Thank you for teaching me how to steward what God's actually put in my heart and to be faithful and obedient wherever I am. You have taught me so much about putting my own agenda for my life on the burner to let God take control. I have cried with you more than any person on this earth. You have seen me at my absolute lowest and have chosen me still. I don't know why God entrusted me with a friend like you, but I'm sure grateful He did. I'll never tire of thanking Him for it. Thanks for being the best travel companion, the one who says, "No Cav, you're being ridiculous … Do this," and, in a second, weight immediately lifts off my shoulders. You have a different sightline than I do and scope with which you see, and I am incredibly grateful for it. You have truly helped mold me into a strong man by simply being you.

Zsanae, last but most certainly not least … Nae, I sure love you. Thank you for living out honor in about every way I know. You are so quick to jump in and be the hands and feet of Jesus wherever you are. Your bravery to go out into the world to do and be exactly who God has called you to be is nothing short of inspiring. Nothing is too difficult for you, and no mountain is too high for you to scale for those you love. I have firsthand experience with that reality. Thank you for always being willing to "go there" with me, for watching musicals with me and letting me geek out and tell you why I love them, for crying with me and hearing my heart, for having difficult conversations and not running from them, but most importantly for giving me the best laugh I've ever had in my life...cut to the river about 5 years ago "Help … Help. A little help please."

ENDNOTES

2 ... THE HARD CHAPTER

1   Proverbs 6:16–19
2   2 Corinthians 12:7–11
3   Romans 3:23–24
4   1 Corinthians 10:13; Proverbs 7:25–26
5   https://www.youtube.com/watch?v=0B_lnQIITxU

3 ... RELATIONSHIPS AND OTHER IDOLS

6   Matthew 10:5–8
7   Isaiah 55:8–9
8   1 Samuel 16:7
9   Romans 5:8
10 John 3:16
11 Galatians 2:20
12 Ephesians 2:8, Galatians 2:20
13 Philippians 4:19
14 1 John 4:7–21
15 Matthew 22:37; Mark 12:30–31; Luke 10:27
16 Matthew 5:21–22
17 1 Corinthians 15:57
18 Psalm 119; John 6:63
19 Hebrews 10:1–18; John 19:28–30
20 Isaiah 9:6–7

21   Genesis 22

22   Romans 8:28

23   Galatians 3:26; 1 John 3; John 1:12; John 15:15; Romans 8:1–3

24   Ezekiel 36:25–26; Hebrews 9:13–14; 1 John 1:7

25   Galatians 3:13; Isaiah 44:22; Romans 5:1; Romans 3:21–26;
      Romans 15:7

26   Ephesians 2:9; Romans 8:17; Hebrews 10:10

27   1 Corinthians 15:57

28   2 Corinthians 5:17; Galatians 2:20

29   John 15:15; Romans 6:6

30   Romans 8:1–3; Ephesians 1:3

31   1 Peter 2:9; Colossians 1:22; Hebrews 10:17; Ephesians 1:7–8;
      1 John 1:9

32   Ephesians 2:6

33   Ephesians 2:10

34   1 Corinthians 12:27; 2 Corinthians 1:20

35   Proverbs 3:26; Proverbs 14:26; 1 John 5:14; Proverbs 28:1;
      Ephesians 2:19

36   Colossians 2:10; Philippians 4:7

37   Ephesians 5:25–26

38   Ephesians 5:26; Romans 12:2

4 ... THE STRENGTH OF SURRENDER

39   Mark 8:36–37

40   2 Peter 1:3; Romans 10:2

41   James 1:17; Psalm 52:1, 145:9

42   Philippians 1:21
43   Isaiah 30:15
44   Romans 8:31–38
45   Psalm 19
46   Matthew 7:7

5 ... GRACE RECEIVED = GRACE TO GIVE
47   Romans 3:25; Romans 5:8–9; Ephesians 1:7; Hebrews 10:12–14
48   Psalm 3:3
49   Proverbs 18:24
50   Ephesians 4:26–27
51   1 Corinthians 13

6 ... UNMASKING THE LIE OF YESTERDAY
52   Luke 3:5
53   Romans 5:6–8
54   Romans 3:21–4:8; Galatians 3:13; Hebrews 7:27
55   Psalm 138:8

7 ... RE-SEEING HOW YOU SEE
56   Ephesians 6:12
57   Ephesians 2:10, 4:1; Romans 1:6, 8:30; Isaiah 43:1
58   Psalm 107:1, 119:68, 145:9; Matthew 19:16–17
59   Psalm 31:19, 34:8, 84:11; 1 Timothy 4:4; James 1:17;
      Romans 2:4, 8:28; 2 Peter 1:3

60   Psalm 33:4; Proverbs 30:5; Isaiah 40:8; Matthew 24:35;
      Luke 1:37; 2 Timothy 2:13
61   Isaiah 40:28, 55:8–9; Job 26:14; Psalm 8:3–4, 147:5;
      Deuteronomy 10:17
62   Jeremiah 29:11

8 ... TO KNOW AND BE KNOWN
63   Proverbs 21:2; John 2:24–25; Psalm 44:21
64   1 Corinthians 3:11–15

9 ... LIFE, LIBERTY, AND THE PURSUIT OF PURPOSE
65   Romans 8:28
66   Philippians 2:12
67   John 10:27–30; Psalm 32:8

10 ... THE ASK
68   Romans 7:15–25
69   Romans 4:16–22
70   John 10:10
71   Ephesians 3:20–21
72   John 13:34, 15:12
73   Romans 2:4; Psalm 18:35, 93:4, 94:18
74   Joshua 1:5, 9
75   Psalm 143:8, Isaiah 49:16
76   Ephesians 2:19–22; Isaiah 41:13

77 John 15:13; Psalm 118:22, Matthew 21:42; Acts 4:11; Romans 9:33; 1 Peter 2:4

78 Matthew 10:32

79 John 3:16–17

80 Romans 5:9

81 Galatians 2:20

82 1 Peter 1:16; Romans 12:2